1,001 things you **must do** before you get **married**

Author's acknowledgements

Thanks to all the girls I've loved before: you made researching this book so much fun. To Nick and Jim for helping me out with some X-rated research: shame some of it just needed too many Xs! To Pug: Easy, tiger. To David: for making it (mostly) legal. To Martin: Meeeeeooowww! And, of course, to Wendy.

This edition published in 2001

10 9 8 7 6 5 4 3 2 1

A CIP catalogue record for this book is available from the British Library

ISBN 1 84222 402 6

Project editor: Martin Corteel
Project art direction: Mark Lloyd
Production: Lisa French
Cartoonist: Nicola Slater
Printed in Great Britain

1,001 things you
must do before
you get married

John Mullet

CARLTON
BOOKS

INTRODUCTION

Getting married? Fine. Good for you.

Worried that those halcyon days of slobbing out, shouting at the TV in a drunken daze while you drool into an empty pizza box, will soon be over? You should be, because if you think the missus is going to put up with that kind of stuff you've got another think coming. Gone will be the extended Friday night benders that finish in time for kick-off on Saturday afternoon, as will be the thrill of giving some old chat to the top barmaid at the Dog and Duck on a Sunday lunchtime. Also gone will be the dubious thrill of wearing the same pants every day for a week – so maybe it's not all bad.

In place of these established hunter/gatherer male rituals will come nights in with the wife watching the weepie on the box, regular dinner at the in-laws' and – gasp – even food shopping at the supermarket on a regular basis (beer and pasty frenzies don't count).

So as the Big Day draws near and she's busy sorting out the disco and trying to persuade cousin Darren to turn up even though you threw up on the vicar at his wedding, you'll need to engage in some extra-curricular activity to take your mind off things and above all to make sure that once you're hitched you don't spend a moment thinking of all the things you should have done when you were a free man. This book offers you ideas of all kinds to celebrate your masculinity while you still have a chance.

Think of this book as your guide, your friend, and maybe even as an accompaniment to the little voice in your head that says "go on, you only live once".

And remember the longest sentence in the English language:

Will you marry me?

X-RATINGS

The X-ratings attached to each item are indicators of how much fun, how dangerous, how erotic and – in some cases – how downright silly each activity is.

A single X means that it's pretty mellow, performable on a Sunday afternoon or in front of your parents, whereas XXXXX means you might pull a muscle(!), contract a social disease or even end up on the run from the law. A dash means that there is no particular risk – physical, mental or legal – but it is something that should be done.

Don't say you weren't warned!

1   X-RATING **XX**

Go to a show at the Folies Bergères.

32, rue Richter,
75009, Paris.
Tel: 00 33 1 44 79 98 98.
Métro: Cadet, rue Montmartre.

2   X-RATING **X**

Drink champagne for breakfast at Tiffany's.

3   X-RATING **XXX**

Join the 'mile high' club.

Let's not get confused: Mile High Club refers
to two people engaging in sexual activity at an altitude
of no less than 5,280 ft (a mile above the earth) in an airplane.

4   X-RATING **XXXXX**

See *Deep Throat*… with a friend.

5 | **X-RATING XXX**

Go clubbing in Ibiza. And score two birds with one stone by visiting:

http://www.ibiza-bangkok.com. First ogle, then book your ticket.

6 | **X-RATING XXXX**

Go to a massage parlour in Bangkok.

7 | **X-RATING XXXXX**

Give your girlfriend a vibrator for Valentine's day.

www.adultsextoysuk.co.uk is the place to go,
with their microwavable 'Hot Cock', or the Fire Fly
Ecstasy Made Easy that rotates, vibrates and wiggles.

8 | **X-RATING X**

Go backpacking in Nepal.

Once you're there it is cheap: US$5 (£3.50) for a two-hour elephant ride in the jungle; beer at 50 cents (35p) a bottle; US$30 (£22) for a two-day white water rafting trip; the priciest fine dining just US$3 (£1.70) per person…

All because the lady loves …

9
X-RATING XXXX

Go window shopping in Amsterdam's red light district.

www.hipplanet.com/amsterdam/redlight.htm.

10
X-RATING X

Go on safari to Kenya.

Wildlife Safari Kenya Limited
International House
PO Box 56803
Nairobi, Kenya
Tel: 00 254 2 340319 or 220747.

11
X-RATING XXX

Go to a pole-dancing club.

12
X-RATING X

See a football match at the Theatre of Dreams.

Old Trafford has been the focus for the passion of millions of
fans around the world for nearly 90 years.
Treat yourself to a day tour through www.manutd.com.

13   X-RATING **XXX**

Do a ton-up on a motorbike.

14   X-RATING **XXX**

Take out a subscription to *Penthouse*.

Details from the top shelf of your local newsagent.

15   X-RATING **X**

Heckle a stand-up comedian.

16   X-RATING **———**

Drive a Porsche.

Porsche 911 Targa 1987, removable centre roof section – finished in bright red with black leather interior – the ultimate German sportscar? Seats 2+2 small. www.classic-car-hire.co.uk.

17
X-RATING **X**

Climb Ben Nevis.

18
X-RATING ——

Win a teddy bear at a funfair
(then give it to a small child).

19
X-RATING **X**

Get as close as possible to the edge at the
top of the Empire State Building.

*Earn it: Australian Paul Crake broke his own record by winning the 24th Annual
Empire State Building Run-Up on February 7, 2001. The 1999 and 2000
Men's Winner finished in 9 minutes 37 seconds, breaking the record
he set a year earlier. Can you do better?*

20
X-RATING **XX**

Go diving (and loco!) at Acapulco.

21   X-RATING X

Appear on Blind Date (but put your name down for Mr & Mrs!).

'She is going to be one of the biggest stars in this country for thirty or forty years' (Brian Epstein, manager of Cilla Black and the Beatles). Check out www.cillablack.com to know what to deal with.

22   X-RATING X

Eat smoked salmon and caviar at the Ritz.

Caviar should be served with a non-metallic spoon, usually mother of pearl, bone or horn. Use plain white (thin) bread toasted (crusts removed), unsalted butter or petit toast or blinis.

23   X-RATING ——

Grow a goatee beard.

24   X-RATING X

Drink a 25-year-old malt whisky.

One such is Laphroaig. Try it with a log fire roaring and your girlfriend sprawled on a dead animal rug on the floor.

25

X-RATING **XXX**

Have a dirty weekend in Brighton.

26

X-RATING **XX**

Go on a pub crawl in Dublin.

Visit Mulligan's of Poolbeg Street for possibly the best pint of Guinness in the world.

27

X-RATING **X**

Watch World Championship Darts at Frimley Green.

28

X-RATING **XXXXX**

Have a skinhead haircut.

While you're at it, get yourself a pair of Classic 8-eyelet Dr Martens boots, available in sizes 2–15 (half sizes 13.5–14.5), made from selected leathers and in many styles: Saddle, Shimmer, Smooth, Abilene, Aniline, Grizzly, New West, Commando Waxi Suede, Crazy horse, Cyclone, Granada, Greasy and Patent.

29

X-RATING **XXXX**

Buy a blow-up doll.

30

X-RATING XX

Sing 'My Way' (Sid's version) at a karaoke night.

If you're feeling shy, just buy your own system at
www.community.chester.pa.us.

31

X-RATING XXXX

Play strip poker with your girlfriend and her
best friend (or sister).

32

X-RATING X

Go racing at the Prix de l'Arc de Triomphe.

Held on the first Sunday in October at Longchamp racecourse in
the Bois de Boulogne in Paris,

33

X-RATING XX

Fly a helicopter.

Or buy your own! A second-hand 1996 PZL-Swidnik W-3A Sokol
12-seater will cost around $2,100,000 (£1,300,000).

34   X-RATING XXX

Streak across a cricket pitch.

35   X-RATING XX

Go whitewater rafting in the Colorado river at the bottom of the Grand Canyon.

www.rafting-colorado.net
367.55 miles north-east of Los Angeles, California, USA.
Lon: 112W 26' 03", lat: 36N 13' 26" – get there with your GPS.

36   X-RATING X

Install remote-controlled curtains.

37   X-RATING XXX

Attend a vicars and tarts party.

38 X-RATING **X**

See your team win the FA Cup Final.

(If you wait for England to win anything you'll never get married!)

39 X-RATING **XX**

Drink a yard of ale.

40 X-RATING **XXX**

Attend a wine-tasting session.

41 X-RATING **XXX**

Go on a date with a TV personality.

42 X-RATING **XXXXX**

Read the *Kama Sutra* (then put it into practice).

Show the kids how it was done in your day.

43 **X-RATING X**

Go gambling at Monte Carlo.

Monaco is 0.75 sq miles in area and has one of the highest population densities of any country in the world: 42,809 per sq mile.

44 **X-RATING X**

Be top of the squash ladder.

45 **X-RATING X**

Own a greyhound.

Walthamstow Stadium Greyhound Track, Walthamstow, London E17. Victoria tube line & overground railway on the Liverpool St to Chingford line. Buses 97, 357, 215, W11 (N38 nightbus), Evening race meetings every Tuesday, Thursday & Saturday. General Enquiries: 020 8498 3300.

46 **X-RATING XXXX**

Join a rock 'n' roll band.

When you're done, go to www.shopzerogravity.com/pages/fdetox.htm and place an online order for detox products.

47 X-RATING **X**

Run the London Marathon.

The London Marathon uses 88lbs (40kg) of petroleum jelly, 23,000 yards of barriers, 66 gallons of blue line paint and 500 stretchers.

48 X-RATING **XXXX**

Have a 'Taylforth' in a layby.

49 X-RATING **XX**

Light a fart.

Fart gasses have methane in them (the same methane said to be responsible for ozone layer depletion). Methane is highly combustible. Take a tip from a pro: keep your trousers on and don't bend down too far to look – singed hair (whatever type) is both painful and smelly.

50 X-RATING **X**

Wear a pair of Ray-Bans on the front at St-Tropez.

51

X-RATING XXX

Visit the Pamela Anderson website
(don't call her babe!).

At www.pamwatch.com you can learn that Pamela's favourite number is
eleven. Alternatively, visit www.bigtits-galore.com.

52

X-RATING X

Go to a football match with your face painted
in your team colours.

53

X-RATING ——

Get a letter published in *The Times*.

The Letters Editor
The Times
1 Pennington Street
London E98 1TA
Tel: 020 7782 5000.
Fax: 020 7782 5046
Email: letters@thetimes.co.uk.

54   X-RATING **XXX**

Watch an X-rated movie in a hotel bedroom.

*You'll have to be careful if you're on a business trip however –
bills are itemized these days.*

55   X-RATING **X**

Have a go on a dune buggy in Dubai.

*'Drive a 4X4, see some belly dancing, learn the way of the Bedouins
and then sleep in the imposing silence of the desert. Magical.'*

56   X-RATING **X**

Go hang-gliding in Lanzarote.

57   X-RATING **XXX**

Get a hand-job from a harpist.

58

X-RATING X

Cheer on your horse to victory with cries of 'Go on my son' at the Cheltenham Gold Cup.

The Cheltenham Festival takes place (weather and disease permitting) in the middle of March at Cheltenham racecourse, Gloucestershire.

59

X-RATING XXX

Have a slow dance with a PE teacher.

60

X-RATING XXX

Get front-row seats at a female mud-wrestling contest.

To build your own mud-wrestling pit you will need: 4,050 bales of hay, six queen-size mattresses, a sheet of plastic large enough to cover the entire ring and one pickup truck bed load of pre-screened topsoil. Dig a hole, arrange the hay around it, put the mattresses in it, add the soil and water, bring your female friends and enjoy.

61

X-RATING X

Go skiing at Aspen, Colorado.

62   X-RATING ———

Visit Disneyland

The easiest way to plan your trip and book your ticket is online at www.disneyland.com. This is the California resort. The one in Florida is called Walt Disney World.

63   X-RATING ———

Own a set of cordless headphones.

Phillips HC8300FM FM Cordless headphones: £39.99 from Curry's.

64   X-RATING X

Drive a bus.

65   X-RATING XXX

Have a pillow fight at a pyjama party with a girl in a teddy.

Or do it with the neighbours: the Kenwood Volunteer Fire Department organizes the Annual World Pillow Fight Championship in July.
Plaza Park
Warm Springs Road
Kenwood
California, USA.

66 X-RATING **X**

Play pinball in a Parisian bar.

67 X-RATING ———

Build an Airfix Spitfire.

The Spitfire, designed by R J Mitchell, was originally intended as a short range fighter, primarily for defensive duties. The basic Airfix model has 43 pieces and is for skill level 2 – Pretty easy.

68 X-RATING **XX**

Win Monopoly by cheating – preferably strip Monopoly.

69 X-RATING **X**

Grow a moustache.

70

X-RATING **X**

Gatecrash the Glastonbury Festival.

Well, not in 2001, as there won't be one. Michael Eavis issued the following statement on January 4, 2001: 'After much deliberation and consultation I have now decided not to run the Festival this year. There are many good reasons for this.' Have to wait, then.

71

X-RATING **X**

Wear a gold medallion with a shirt open to the waist.

www.rustyzipper.com is the place to go to get your hands on a wonderful shiny disco shirt or some fantastic flares.

72

X-RATING **XXX**

Wear your girlfriend's knickers for a day.

73

X-RATING **XX**

Play Postman's Knock.

Damn! I'm lookin' good.

74

X-RATING **XXX**

Engage in an X-rated email
session with a workmate.

75

X-RATING **X**

Ride a BMX bike.

*Don't try to emulate Dave Mirra, who was hit by a car in 1993
(dislocated shoulder, blood-clot in the brain). Then, in 1995, he
crashed and had to have his spleen removed. He was told that he
would not be able to ride his bike again, but he proved the doctors
wrong. Dave was dubbed the 'Miracle Boy' and continues to impress.*

76

X-RATING **X**

Drive on Route 66.

*(Historic) Route 66 is the (grand)mother of the roads in America.
Once it was the only road crossing the States from the West to
the East Coast, but now it is hardly used as new, more direct
roads have been built. Drive it preferably at the wheel of a
Pontiac Firebird or, of course, a Harley–Davidson.*

77 X-RATING XX

Buy a pack of king-size Rizlas
(with a sense of purpose).

They come in three colours: red, blue and green, and range from medium burn rate to self-extinguishing. Get yourself a 'kingskin' rolling machine too.

78 X-RATING X

Go gliding in Norfolk.

79 X-RATING XX

Get up at 4am to go looking for magic mushrooms.

Magic mushrooms are hallucinogenic, normally psilocybin mushrooms, which contain traces of psilocin, a hallucinogenic drug. The most commonly found 'magic' mushroom in Britain is the Psilocybe Semilanceata *or Liberty Cap mushroom.*

80 X-RATING XXX

Sign up for an escort agency.

Earn from £140 per hour, if you know where to look.

81   X-RATING **XX**

Get into a cinema for nothing through the back door.

82   X-RATING **XX**

Go skinny-dipping at midnight.

Do it on the legendary naturist beach at l'Ile du Levant in France (83400 Ile du Levant, shuttles many times a day from Hyères – around 45 minutes' crossing).

83   X-RATING **XXX**

Have sex in the bath.

84   X-RATING **XX**

Have a piggy-back race up the high street on Saturday afternoon.

The Metropolitan Police Service invests approximately 3 per cent of its total resources (over £32 million) in road policing. Do you really want to add to the problem?

85

X-RATING X

Acquire a traffic cone.

'The battle against the cones will be long and arduous, but we should be prepared for the great evil that we face'. Get organized and visit www.conewars.co.uk to eradicate traffic cones from Britain.

86

X-RATING XXX

Swing from a chandelier.

87

X-RATING XX

Strip down an engine (and put it back together again).

Or you could try your hand at a 55" x 112" 12,000-piece jigsaw puzzle of the 'Creation of Adam' by Michelangelo, available from Ravensburger at www.ravensburger.com (the site is written in German).

88

X-RATING X

Go to the World Snooker Championships at The Crucible Theatre, Sheffield.

89

X-RATING XX

Give someone chocolates on Valentine's day.

Chocolate contains seratonin, a mood lifting hormone which is naturally produced by the brain when a person is happy as well as theobromine, which reduces stress. The phenylethylamine and the caffeine, as stimulants, will make sure that you can make the most of this uplifted mood!

90

X-RATING XXX

Buy sexy underwear for your girlfriend.

Take your pick at www.aubade.com – one of the most famous French lingerie designers.

91

X-RATING XXXX

Pose nude for a male calendar.

92

X-RATING XXX

Cop off with a groupie.

If you don't have a real groupie available, simply put Frank Zappa's Joe's Garage *on and learn about what really happens backstage.*

93

X-RATING XXX

Visit Stonehenge at the Summer Solstice.

94

X-RATING XX

Have a pint of bitter for breakfast at a London market pub.

This one is, obviously, better at the end of an all-night binge.
Pride of Spitalfields
3 Heneage Street
London E1
Tel: 020 7247 8933.
Underground: Liverpool Street (for Spitalfields,
Brick Lane and Petticoat Lane markets).

95

X-RATING XXX

Claim your car has broken down in a quiet spot when giving your girlfriend a lift home.

96

X-RATING XXX

Remove a stripper's bra.

This will probably cost you a bit extra, or, if you
don't have permission, substantially more.

"Lift receiver and insert coin in slot."

97   X-RATING X

Get a table for two at London's River Café.

Tel: 020 7386 4200.

98   X-RATING XX

Attend the Rangers vs. Celtic Glasgow football derby.

But be very careful who you cheer for!

99   X-RATING XXX

Get thrown out of a nightclub by bouncers.

A black eye is caused by bleeding into the tissue around the eye.
This most often follows trauma. The medical term for this type of
bruising is ecchymosis.

100   X-RATING XXXX

Have sex in a phone box.

101 X-RATING X

Throw Shanghai at darts (that's a single, double and treble of the same number in a visit to the oche).

102 X-RATING XX

Buy a Rolex.

Which one? The Oyster collection? The Daytona? The Cellini collection? Go for the solid 18-carat gold, so no nailbiting decisions there, but is quartz more chic than perpetual?

103 X-RATING X

Go rollerblading in Hyde Park.

104 X-RATING X

Score a hat-trick in a football match.

105 X-RATING XXX

Tell your boss to shove his job up his arse.

Then go to www.fish4jobs.com and hope for the best – unless you have a few seedy details on where he really spent last weekend to send to his wife.

106-115 X-RATING

See the top ten porno films –

106 *Shaving Ryan's Privates* (2000)   **XXXXX**

107 *Animal Farm* (1980)   **XXXXX**

108 *Naughty Blue Knickers* (1981)   **XXXX**

109 *The Story of O* (1975)*o   **XXXXX**

110 *Crimes of Passion* (1984)*o   **XXXXX**

111 *Emmanuelle* (1974)*o   **XXX**

112 *Two Moon Junction* (1988)*o   **XX**

113 *Deep Throat* (1975)   **XX**

114 *The Sex Files* (1988)   **XXXXX**

115 *Pammy's Home Video*   **XXXX**

* DVD   o VHS

116

X-RATING XX

Go snowboarding in the Rockies.

How to boardslide: approach the slide, jump a tad higher than the slide itself, stay flat-based, shoulders towards your back, look to the front of the rail, come out fakie.

117

X-RATING XX

Go down the Panama Canal.

Clement Travel
PO Box 9349
Birmingham B14 5TQ
Tel: 0121 693 7041.

118

X-RATING XX

Have a poster of *the* tennis girl on your wall.

Failing that, Anna Kournikova would do.

119

X-RATING XX

Dance in the fountains in Trafalgar Square on New Year's Eve.

120

X-RATING X

Skim stones on the beach at Hastings.

121

X-RATING X

Throw a stick in a river for a real dog to retrieve.

A Newfoundland is undoubtedly the best breed for this.
It can retrieve more than a stick: it will pull you, your mate,
your dinghy and all your fishing gear out of the water.

122

X-RATING XXXX

Play 'pull-a-pig' with your mates.

123

X-RATING XXX

Attend a May Ball at Oxford

These range from college balls or events at about £33–40 to
Commemoration Balls at £180 for a double ticket. You can also
follow the somewhat dangerous tradition of jumping off
Magdalen Bridge into the river on May Morning.

124

X-RATING X

Hear a nightingale sing in Berkeley Square.

125

X-RATING XX

Toss a caber.

126

X-RATING XX

Go to a boxing match.

Go for the real deal: look for the annual World Senior Amateur Boxing Championships.

127

X-RATING X

Eat roast beef and Yorkshire pudding for Sunday lunch on the Costa Brava.

128

X-RATING XXX

Drive a rally car through the Welsh woods.

129

X-RATING XX

Go first-footing at Hogmanay.

That means having the first drink of the year in a welcoming house on Scottish New Year's Day. The minimum requirement is a bottle of whisky and a bannock of oatcake, although it is traditional to carry a piece of coal. You must also have dark hair, or you won't get it.

130

X-RATING XXX

Ride on the back of a dodgem car

Do whatever you want on your own dodgem track: Reverchon Auto track, ideal for any amusement park. Clearance price (cars extra): £16,000.

131

X-RATING XX

Go to the Milan football derby
(AC Milan vs. Internazionale) at the San Siro
(Stadio Giuseppe Meazza).

132

X-RATING XX

Play roulette at Monte Carlo.

133

X-RATING XXX

Eat raw octopus in Korea.

Don't forget the chili sauce – it serves to paralyze the squirming beast and stops the suckers sticking to your throat on the way down.

134

X-RATING XX

Drink piña colada on Copacabana beach.

Ingredients: 3 oz light rum, 3 tbsp coconut milk, 3 tbsp pineapple, crushed. Mixing instructions: put all ingredients into an electric blender with 2 cups of crushed ice. Blend at a high speed for a short length of time. Strain into a glass and serve with a straw.

135

X-RATING XXX

Give grief to a traffic warden.

You could just go to http://www.stupid.com straight away.

"And stick your ticket where the sun doesn't shine!"

136–145

X-RATING

See the following bands or artists performing live:

136 The Rolling Stones   **XX**

137 Eminem   **XXXXX**

138 The Beastie Boys   **XXXX**

139 U2   **XXX**

140 REM   **XXX**

141 Alice Cooper   **XXXXX**

142 Calexico   **XXX**

'Calexico decided to combine the southwestern feel of the Sonoran desert with their old world, spaghetti western arrangements. The result turned out to be some kind of mariachi-tinged soundtrack that Ennio Morricone would have scored on peyote in the early 60s to a young Cormac McCarthy screenplay.'
www.cityslang.com.

143 Santana   **XXX**

144 Britney Spears (why d'you think?)   **XXXXX**

145 The Happy Mondays.   **XXXX**

146

X-RATING **XX**

Go down the shops on a sitdown lawnmower.

Ryan Tripp, the Lawnmower Boy, left from Salt Lake City, Utah and arrived in Washington D.C. 42 days later, having driven 3,116 miles and setting a world record. He mowed the lawn of the U.S. Capitol Building to help raise money for a child in need of a liver transplant.

147

X-RATING **XX**

Make a techno record.

Try it with Dance Ejay, software that enables you to stick together blocks of pre-recorded rhythms and sounds.
www.jungle.com

148

X-RATING **XX**

Drive a tractor.

149
X-RATING **XX**

Burn your own music CD.

Everyone should have a 'Party CD' the way they used to have a 'Party tape' in the 70s.

150
X-RATING **XX**

Go laser-gunning.

Laser Quest Guildford
The Friary Centre
Commercial Road
Guildford
Surrey GU1 4YX
Tel: 01483 456565.

151
X-RATING **XXXXX**

Have a kinky sex session covered in baby oil.

'Johnson's® Baby Oil is made with pure mineral oil to form a silky barrier to prevent excess moisture loss. It helps soften and protect your baby's delicate skin. It's effective enough for adult use, too.'

152

X-RATING XX

Drink a pint of Guinness at the brewery in Dublin.

*Guinness Storehouse, St James Gate, Dublin 8, Ireland.
Once the largest brewery in the world, the 64-acre site
produces 3¹⁄₂ million pints a day.*

153

X-RATING X

See AS Monaco play football in Monaco.

Stade Louis II, tickets available matchdays. www.asm-foot.mc.

154

X-RATING XXX

Attend a whisky-tasting session.

*www.scotchwhisky.com will give you some ideas: Intense nose,
well integrated, complex, peat-smoke, deep fruitiness (melon balls,
nectarines, over-ripe plums), boiled sweets, cinnamon balls,
scorched wool, smoky, Lapsang Suchong tea, slightly oily.*

155

X-RATING XXX

Own a share in a racehorse.

156

X-RATING **XX**

Spout bollocks at Speaker's Corner.

The Royal Parks and Gardens Regulation Act 1872 allowed a space in the north-eastern corner of Hyde Park to be given over for public speaking.

157

X-RATING **X**

Drink Pimm's at Henley during the Regatta in midsummer.

James Pimm started concocting a digestive tonic in 1840, called Pimm's No. 1, made with various herbs and quinine.

158

X-RATING **X**

Shout 'House' at bingo.

159

X-RATING **XX**

Get a holiday job flipping burgers.

160

X-RATING XXX

Go big truck racing.

With names such as Crypt Keeper, Destroyer, Pure Adrenalin,
Sudden Impact, Predator and Bigfoot, you're in for a treat.
Unfortunately, you will more than likely have to visit the USA to see them.

161

X-RATING XX

Go swimming in the Red Sea.

Water temperatures reach 26°C for most of the Red Sea for
much of the year and often exceed 30°C at the peak of summer.

162

X-RATING XXXXX

Work as a roadie for a heavy metal band.

163

X-RATING XX

Go clay-pigeon shooting.

www.cpsa.co.uk
Clay Pigeon Shooting Association
Bisley Camp
Brookwood
Woking
Surrey GU24 0NP
Tel: 01483 485400.

164
X-RATING **X**

Own a pair of walking poles.

165
X-RATING **XXXXX**

Help burn the Pope in Lewes on November 5.

166
X-RATING **XX**

Play the slots at Caesar's Palace.

3570 Las Vegas Blvd
Las Vegas
NV 89109
USA.
With its 23,000 square foot spa (in the 4.5 acre 'Garden of the Gods' water complex), hundreds of slot machines and its 'insert-a-quarter-and-you-could-win-a-Harley–Davidson' games, there are far less glamorous ways to lose your money.

167

Fire an Uzi.

Caliber: 9mm.
Operation: Blowback, closed breech with floating firing pin.
Barrel: 4.5 inches.
Magazine capacity: 9mm: 20-round
It's absolutely, positively a classic.

168

Have sex in a cornfield.

169

Chat up an airline stewardess.

Could lead to joining the Mile High Club if you're lucky.

"Excuse me, do you have any Mile High Club application forms?"

See the top ten action movies:

170 *The Matrix* (1999)*o **XXX**

'There is a difference between knowing the path and walking the path.'

171 *Scarface* (1983)*o **XXXXX**

'I buried those cockroaches.'

172 *Goodfellas* (1990)*o **XXXXX**

'All my life I wanted to be a gangster.'

173 *Hard Boiled* (1992)*o **XXXXX**

174 *Gladiator* (2000)*o **XXXX**

175 *Die Hard* (1988)*o **XXXX**

176 *Lethal Weapon* (1987)*o **XXXX**

177 *The Man Who Would Be King* (1975)*o **XXX**

178 *Terminator 2: Judgement Day* (1991)o **XXXX**

179 *Midnight Run* (1988)*o **XXX**

*'I've got two words for you. Shut the f**k up.'*

* DVD   o VHS

180
X-RATING XXX

Play craps in a New York casino.

Brooklyn Casino
1540 Flatbush Ave
Brooklyn
USA.

181
X-RATING XXXX

Get a Scottish lassie to toss your caber.

182
X-RATING XXX

Write a love poem and give it to the object
of your desire.

183

X-RATING XXXX

Do a handbrake turn.

Slow the car down to about 20–30 miles per hour in second gear. Dip the clutch and pull the handbrake hard enough to lock both rear wheels. With your remaining hand, steer smoothly in either direction. The car will swing round, pivoting around the front wheels. When the car has nearly gone 180 degrees, straighten the front wheels, release the handbrake and apply the brakes… or put the pedal to the metal for that real Sweeney feeling!

184

X-RATING XXXX

Re-enact the Beatles' famous road-crossing at Abbey Road à la Red Hot Chili Peppers (socks on cocks).

185

X-RATING XX

Visit the World War I battlefields in northern France.

186

X-RATING XXXX

Make a spoof heavy-breathing phone call (and then phone to apologize).

187

X-RATING **XX**

Play football in the park next to a
'No Ball Games' notice.

188

X-RATING **XX**

Eat raw eggs as a hangover cure.

Try the Porto Flip – a glass of Porto with a couple of raw eggs in it.

189

X-RATING **XXX**

Brew your own beer.

190

X-RATING **X**

Eat tapas in Bilbao.

191

X-RATING XX

Watch the sun rise at Ayers Rock.

Ayers Rock, aka Mount Uluru was formed in the beginnings of the Precambrian era, about 550 million years ago. Whole mountain ranges rose and eroded away over the next 200 million years, and produced the Mann, Musgrave and Petermann Ranges in Central Australia.

192

X-RATING XX

Have a scrub at a Turkish Bath.

Ironmonger Row Baths
Ironmonger Row
Islington
London EC1V 3QN
Tel: 020 7253 4011.

193

X-RATING XX

Spend your summer holiday in a cowboy ranch.

American Round-Up
Oxenways
Membury
Axminster
Devon EX13 7JR
Tel: 01404 881777

194

X-RATING XXX

Take a woman for a punt up river.

Have tea at The Orchard in Granchester. Ask the waitress, "Is there honey still for tea?" Then duck – she's heard that joke 500 times a day.

195

X-RATING XX

Go salmon fishing in Scotland.

Fishing Scotland
Roy Bridge
Inverness-shire
Scotland PH31 4AG
Tel: 01397 712812.

196

X-RATING XXX

Get off with an It Girl at a celebrity party.

"Who's your daddy now?"

197

X-RATING **XXXX**

Spend a night in a police cell.

198

X-RATING **XXX**

Pogo at a punk band concert.

Concussion. A concussion is the result of a blow or sudden, uncontrolled, rapid movement to the head. It can cause memory loss, problems with thinking or temporary unconsciousness.

199

X-RATING **XX**

Get into a car through the window.

Do this enough times and you may find Daisy Duke in the passenger seat.

Play the top ten video games:

200	Championship Manager	X
201	Virtual Valerie	XXXXX
202	Resident Evil	XXX
203	Tomb Raider	XXXX

And no, there isn't and never has been a nude patch for Lara Croft. All the ads you find on the web are fake. So forget about it, grab your joystick and be happy with what pixels you have.

204	Oni	XXXX
205	Command & Conquer	XX
206	Starcraft	XX
207	ISS2	XX
208	Unreal Tournament	XXXXX
209	Sensible Soccer	X

210
X-RATING XXX

Go to the supermarket dressed as Tarzan.

211
X-RATING X

Meet an old acquaintance on a lunchtime
perambulation on the Saturday of a
cricket test match at Lord's.

212
X-RATING XXXXX

Ring a hot housewife on a telephone chatline.

www.dirtyhousewives.com.

213
X-RATING X

Run a fantasy football team.

www.telegraphpremierleague.com

214

X-RATING XXX

Lead the conga round a room at a party.

215

X-RATING XXXXX

Buy a blow-up sheep.

Order online from www.muttonbone.com, a site endorsed by PETER, People for the Ethical Treatment of Erotic Ruminants.

216

X-RATING X

Work on a Kibbutz.

Kibbutz Adventure Centre Head Office
66 Ben Yehuda Street
Tel Aviv 63432
Israel.

217

X-RATING XXXX

Get a fraulein to play with your sausage.

218

X-RATING XXXX

Go feting in Trinidad.

'Plenty socca fuh da body, plenty muzik fuh da mind, come a fete in Trinidad'. Quite.

219

X-RATING XX

Drink red wine and coke in a
bar in Las Rambas, Barcelona.

220

X-RATING XXXXX

Have sex on the beach.

You have to remember though that there is only one place where a grain of sand is more irritating than between your teeth...

221

X-RATING XXX

Celebrate All-Saints' Day (November 1) in
Little Italy (New York City).

222 — X-RATING XXXX

Frolic with your girlfriend on a waterbed.

Huxley's Waterbeds
PO Box 29
Crowborough
East Sussex TN6 1WQ.

223 — X-RATING XXX

Play British Bulldog.

224 — X-RATING XXXXX

Buy a pack of novelty condoms… and use them.

Condom Willie Vending Products
PO Box 367
Swardeston
Norwich
Norfolk NR14 8UR.

225 — X-RATING XXXXX

Ride a horse through the desert.

The next best thing would be to wrap a bath towel around your head,
turn the heating on and watch Lawrence of Arabia *on DVD.*

226
X-RATING **XXX**

Travel on the Nile.

227
X-RATING **XXX**

Visit the urinals at the Philharmonic Hotel in Liverpool.

228
X-RATING **X**

Host your own website.

*www.schogini.com offers UK domain names (www.yourname.co.uk)
and hosting services at very competitive prices.*

229
X-RATING **X**

Play boules in Nice.

230
X-RATING **XX**

Attend a Northern Soul all-nighter in Wigan.

231

Slurp oysters à deux.

232

Visit the Valley of the Kings.

233

Have a dirty dance with the head girl.

234

Go to the Mardi Gras in Rio.

235

Buy a case of vintage champagne
from a Champagne House.

Le Champagnes Jardin
3, rue Charpentier Laurain
Le Menil Sur Oger 51190
France.

"So, do you *come* here often?"

236

X-RATING XX

Recite a poem at an open mike evening.

237

X-RATING XXXX

Have a body piercing (ears don't count).

238

X-RATING XX

Watch the girls go by from a Parisian pavement café.

It has *to be on the Champs Elysees.*

239

X-RATING XXXX

Go to a lap-dancing club.

Venus Lap Dancing Club
29–35 Farringdon Road
London EC1M 3JF
Tel: 020 7242 1571.

240

X-RATING X

Make a prediction on Groundhog Day in Puxatawney.

241

X-RATING **XX**

Play bar football in a Marseille café.

ASBM (Association Sportive de Baby-Foot Marseillais)
Escale Hopkinson
52 rue Beau
Marseille 13004
France.

242

X-RATING **XXX**

Walk the Pennine Way.

243

X-RATING **X**

Re-enact a Civil War battle.

www.englishcivilwar.com
The Sealed Knot Society
Tel: 01928 701603.

244

X-RATING **XXX**

Rub shoe polish on the receiver of a public telephone.

245

X-RATING XXXX

Have sex in a log cabin.

246

X-RATING XX

Go go-karting.

Streatham Kart Raceway
390 Streatham High Road
London SW16 6HX
Tel: 020 8677 8677.

247

X-RATING XXX

Chat up a pretty woman at an art gallery.

This has to be done the right way, i.e. by saying something very deep
or meaningful in front of a painting at the Tate Modern. Or you could
try 'interesting' facts, for instance, that the Bankside Power Station is
made of more than 4.2 million bricks, or that the height of the central
chimney was brought down to 325 ft so that it was lower than the
dome of St Paul's Cathedral.

248

X-RATING XXX

Go to a bellydancing club.

Want to practice Raqs Sharqi? Then go to:
The Factory Fitness and Dance Centre
407 Hornsey Road
London N19.

249   X-RATING **XX**

Drink a late-night coffee at Bar Italia in Soho.

Bar Italia
22 Frith St
London W1D 4RP
Tel: 020 7437 4520.

250   X-RATING **XX**

Get a holiday job in a bar.

251   X-RATING **XXXX**

Go moose hunting.

252   X-RATING **XXX**

Ride a snowmobile.

253   X-RATING **XXX**

Play dominoes in a Barbados rum shop.

254

X-RATING XXX

Chat up a girl in a foreign language.

www.berlitz.com.

255

X-RATING XX

Go scuba diving.

256

X-RATING XXX

Eat haggis and drink whisky on Burns Night.

January 25, the birthday of Scotland's national poet, Robert Burns (1759–1796).

257

X-RATING XXX

Go to fashion week at Milan.

258

X-RATING XX

Blow the whistle for departure on a train station platform.

259

X-RATING XXXXX

Read the dirty bits of the work of the Marquis de Sade.

The Misfortunes of Virtue and Other Early Tales *by the Marquis de Sade.*
www.amazon.co.uk

260

X-RATING X

Play the saxophone.

261

X-RATING XXX

Unhook a girl's bra with one hand.

262

X-RATING XX

Drive a Rolls Royce.

263

X-RATING XX

Celebrate Chinese New Year in Chinatown.

264

X-RATING XX

Have champagne and ice cream in a café on Nevsky Prospekt, St. Petersburg.

Alexander Dumas called Nevsky 'the street of religious tolerance', because of the many churches of various faiths you can find there.

265

X-RATING XX

Go jet-skiing in Australia.

266

X-RATING XXX

Roller-skate round Paris on a Saturday night.

For French emergency services dial 12.

267

X-RATING XXX

Go on a booze cruise to Calais.

SeaFrance Eastern Docks
Dover
Kent CT16 1JA
Tel: 08705 711711.

268

X-RATING **XX**

See the musical *Hair*.

This is the dawning of the Age of Aquarius after all.

269

X-RATING **XX**

Drink sherry in Jerez.

King Henry I proposed an arrangement with the inhabitants of Bordeaux: their wine in exchange for English wool, in order to develop both sectors. The French refused, but the Jerezians did accept the offer.

270

X-RATING **XXX**

Set off big fireworks on Guy Fawkes Night.

271

X-RATING **XXXXX**

Go on a Club 18–30 holiday.

272

X-RATING **XXXX**

Do a runner from a restaurant leaving your mates to pay.

Ronnie's indigestion tablets will come in useful –
as will a new set of friends!

273
X-RATING XX

Go on a Beaujolais Nouveau run.

On the second Thursday of November each year.

274
X-RATING XXXX

Have a day shooting your mates with realistic airsoft guns.

www.airsoft.com.

275
X-RATING XXX

Take a sleigh ride in the snow with a chalet girl.

276
X-RATING XX

Carry a flaming torch at Up Helly Aa in Lerwick, Orkney Islands.

277
X-RATING XXXX

Fly a microlight.

278 — X-RATING XX

Watch the sun go down in Montego Bay.

www.jamaicatravel.com.

279 — X-RATING XXXXX

Take Greyhound buses from New York to Los Angeles.

Departure 03:45. Arrival 20:55. Total time: 2 days, 20 hours, 10 minutes for a total of 3,079 miles. Fare: US$144 (£104). www.greyhound.com

280 — X-RATING XXXX

Have a doomed holiday romance.

281 — X-RATING XXX

Go elephant riding.

282 — X-RATING XXXX

Ride a tandem behind a girl in hot pants.

283 — X-RATING XXXX

Make love on a fur rug in front of a log fire.

284 — X-RATING XXXXX

Collect erotic Japanese prints.

These are called shungas (dating from the 1700s) and can get pretty expensive if old. You could do worse than buying Mangas instead.

285 — X-RATING X

Have a shave at a London city barbers.

286 — X-RATING XX

Walk up all the steps at Mont St Michel.

287 — X-RATING XXX

Frolic in the Forum in Rome.

288

X-RATING XXX

French kiss a girl on the metro in Paris.

The equivalent of a 'French letter' in French is an 'English coat'.

289

X-RATING XXXX

Have a poolside toe-sucking session.

290

X-RATING XXXXX

Play doctors and nurses at a trainee nurses' party.

291

X-RATING XXXXX

Go surfing in Newquay.

Before you go, check out the waves from:
www.headlandhotel.co.uk/surfcam/surfcam.html.
There they update images of the state of the sea every hour.

292

X-RATING **XXXX**

 Ride the biggest roller coaster at Alton Towers.

The Nemesis promises you will experience G-forces of 4 (a US space shuttle at take off reaches G-force 3), total weightlessness and speeds of up to 50mph.

293

X-RATING **XXXXX**

Have a girl in stiletto heels walk across your bare back.

294

X-RATING **XXX**

Goose a girl at the Nottingham Goose Fair.

'He who eats goose on Michaelmas day shan't money lack or debts to pay.'

295

X-RATING **XXX**

Drink a Bollicker in Antwerp.

Preferably at the temple of Belgian beer:
The Kulminator,
32 Vlemickveld,
Antwerp (Anvers)
Belgium.

296

X-RATING XXX

Twist and shout with a girl in bobby sox and a ra-ra skirt.

297

X-RATING XX

Buy a pair of handmade shoes.

298

X-RATING XXXX

Play grown-up kiss chase.

299

X-RATING XXXXX

Tie your girlfriend to a four-poster bed (make sure she's up for it first)

The Four Poster Bed Company
Widgeon Hill
Hamnish
Leominster
Worcestershire HR6 0QN
Tel: 01568 760 622.

"Ouch! What a prick."

300

X-RATING XXXX

Play the Sex board game.

301

X-RATING X

Impersonate Michael Flatley at the Fleadh,
Finsbury Park, London.

302

X-RATING XXX

Attend a bullfight in Seville.

303

X-RATING XXXX

Enjoy fellatio with a flautist.

*To book a classical artist, for any type of function, try www.musiclink.co.uk,
for all your musical needs.*

304

X-RATING XXXX

Sing 'Four and Twenty Virgins' on a rugby club tour.

Find the full lyrics at http://members.aol.com/llewtrah/.

305

X-RATING XXX

Skive off work and go to Royal Ascot.

306

X-RATING XXXX

Go camping alone after watching *Deliverance*.

Directed by John Boorman in 1972, this is the story of four friends on a canoeing trip in the deep south of the USA and contains scenes of buggery and other unpleasantness. Available on VHS and DVD.

307

X-RATING XXXX

Party with a Valley Girl.

I found this guy, oh my Gawd, like, TOTALLY awesome. He was reading this book y'know, bitchin' cool and I wanted to take him back to Cal with me cuz he was a real pup like, gag me with a spoon! But he was getting married to a grody English chick who looked TOTALLY like she'd never seen a nail polish parlour in her life, I mean, grody to the max... whatever!

308

X-RATING XXXXX

Have an ill-advised one-night stand with a workmate.

Get your Premium Divorce LegalPac, only valid in England and Wales, for £80 from www.divorce-online.co.uk.

309

X-RATING XX

Construct a piece of Art in your back garden.

310

X-RATING XXXXX

Have sex on your boss's desk.

Be sure to remove all metallic objects, such as belt buckles, rings, jewellery and beware not to scratch the mahogany surface with your trouser zip or her nails.

311

X-RATING XXXX

Play pool in a Chicago poolhouse.

312

X-RATING XXX

Send flowers to someone you've always fancied on Valentine's day.

www.interflora.co.uk.

313

X-RATING XXXX

Have sex in the shower.

314

X-RATING **XXXX**

Deface an advertising hoarding.

315

X-RATING **XXXXX**

Take the starring role in a home porno movie.

316

X-RATING **XXXXX**

Have cyber sex.

'FuckU-FuckMe™ provides the most complete remote sex solution for the Internet and corporate intranet. Powerful features let you sexually communicate with your remote partner and provide an absolutely realistic sensual experience of real intercourse.' www.fu-fme.com.

317

X-RATING **XXXXX**

Play a round of golf at St Andrews.

www.standrews.org.uk
Tel: 01334 477036.

318

X-RATING ——

Kiss the Blarney Stone.

319

X-RATING XXX

Spit on the Heart of Midlothian.

Heart of Midlothian FC
Tynecastle Stadium
Gorgie Road
Edinburgh EH11 2NL.

320

X-RATING X

Throw coins in the Trevi Fountain.

Trevi fountain, built between 1732 and 1751 by architects Pietro da
Cortona, Bernini and Nicola Salvi in Rome, Italy, is probably the most
famous fountain in the world. Throwing coins in it ensures the usual
amount of luck, love and prosperity for the rest of year.

321

X-RATING X

Have your hair cut at Vidal Sassoon.

322

X-RATING X

Collect saucy seaside postcards.

323   X-RATING **X**

Buy a bespoke suit from a Jermyn Street tailor.

Nearest Tube Stations: Piccadilly Circus (Bakerloo and Piccadilly Lines –
just 75 yards from Jermyn Street); Green Park (Jubilee, Piccadilly
and Victoria Lines – 3–4 minutes' walk to Jermyn Street).

324   X-RATING **XXXX**

Rattle a flamenco dancer's castanets in Cordoba.

325   X-RATING **XX**

See the movie, but *do not* talk about *Fight Club*.

326   X-RATING **XXX**

Play poker all night with the lads.

327   X-RATING **XXXXX**

Have a stripper wriggle on your knee.

328

X-RATING XXXXX

Go joyriding.

Don't pretend you weren't warned though: joyriding is an offence and will get you into trouble.

329

X-RATING XXXXX

Have a sex session with a woman in a basque.

330

X-RATING XXX

Spend a day at work making paper airplanes.

331

X-RATING XXXX

Take nude photos of your girlfriend.

*What you do with them afterwards is a matter for your conscience…
There is little chance, however, that she will ever look at soft porn Internet sites that welcome this kind of amateur contribution. Think about it.*

332

X-RATING XXX

Have an account at a bookmakers.

333

X-RATING **X**

Watch tennis on the Centre Court at Wimbledon.

334

X-RATING **XXXX**

Get an English rose to spin round your Maypole.

335

X-RATING **XXX**

Carve your name on a park bench.

336

X-RATING **XXXX**

Spray graffiti.

And clean it up with Resolv Plus, an advanced formula gel especially developed to remove old graffiti, residual staining and leather dyes from non- or semi-porous surfaces.
Graffiti Solutions: 01273 857785.

337

X-RATING **XX**

Join a betting syndicate.

Make the world a brighter place.

338

X-RATING XX

Go grape-picking in southern France.

Come the end of August, early September and the whole of France will get ready for 'les vendanges', or grape-picking season. You can travel to the south of France and get a job there easily. The work is gruesome, back-shattering and the money is poor, but what stands it apart is the fantastic ambiance, the singing, the communal life and, of course, the wine.

339

X-RATING XXX

Wolf-whistle a nubile passer-by from a building site.

340

X-RATING XX

Have a tailgate party in the Twickenham Stadium car park.

*Twickenham Stadium
Rugby Road
Twickenham
Middlesex TW1 1DZ
Tel: 020 8891 4565.*

341

X-RATING XXX

Ask people for change on the London Underground.

342 X-RATING **XX**

Dye your hair yellow.

343 X-RATING **XXXX**

Puke in your shoes.

Buy yourself a spray can of Scholl Odour Control Foot Spray (200ml), around £2.50 from your local chemist.

344 X-RATING **XXXX**

Fart loudly at a dinner party (if it's at your prospective in-laws it may render this book pointless).

345 X-RATING **XXXXX**

Invade the pitch at a football match.

It is illegal and if you are caught, you will probably be arrested, miss the rest of the game and probably every other one for a long time.

346 X-RATING XX

Vomit off the side of a boat (not at the Boat Show).

Seasickness is caused by the body, inner ear, and eyes all sending different signals to the brain, resulting in confusion and queasiness. It is a problem generally attributed to disturbance in the balance system of the inner ear (vestibular) system. Your sensory perception gets out of synch as these nerve fibres attempt to compensate for the unfamiliar motion of the ship moving through water.

347 X-RATING XXXXX

Shag a bridesmaid at your mate's wedding.

348 X-RATING XX

Go singing – and dancing – in the rain.

Alternatively, stay indoors and watch Gene Kelly do his umbrella and splashes trick from your sofa (after all, Kelly had a 103-degree fever when he danced to the title song).

349 X-RATING XXXX

Have an affair with an older woman.

350

X-RATING **XXX**

Book into a motel with your girlfriend as
Mr & Mrs Smith.

351

X-RATING **XX**

Carry a bag for a girl you fancy.

352

X-RATING **XXXX**

Ask a waitress back to your place at closing time.

353

X-RATING **XXX**

Wear a 46DD bra as ear-muffs.

354

X-RATING **XXXXX**

Eat 50 hard-boiled eggs in an hour.

355

X-RATING XXXXX

Drive a woman to the height of screaming ecstasy in bed.

356

X-RATING XXXX

Make passes at women who wear glasses.

357

X-RATING XXXX

Say 'nice beaver' to a woman on a ladder.

358

X-RATING XXXX

Do some twosome clay-modelling on a wheel with a fit art teacher.

Don't forget to watch Ghost *first.*

359

X-RATING XXXXX

Make love under a ceiling mirror.

360

X-RATING X

Sleep in a hammock.

The Mexican Hammock Co.
42 Beauchamp Road
Bristol BS7 8LQ
Tel: 0117 942 5353.

361

X-RATING XXX

Proposition a girl in a phone bar restaurant.

362

X-RATING XXXX

Shag a woman for a bet.

363

X-RATING XXX

Play Knock-down Ginger.

364

X-RATING XXXX

Send a risqué text message to a woman you fancy.

www.textmessenger.co.uk

365

X-RATING XXXX

Cavort with a strip-a-gram policewoman.

366

X-RATING XXXX

Ski off-piste.

To ski off-piste is to ski outside the standard ski tracks arranged by skiing resorts. This is more fun, but also more dangerous. Do it with class at Courchevel, in the French Savoie region.

367

X-RATING XXXXX

Be guest of honour at a girl-on-girl sex session.

368

X-RATING XXXXX

Do 'the Full Monty' to gasps of admiration from the female audience.

369   X-RATING XXX

Go to a Marilyn Manson concert.

Check out http://marilynmansondirect.com first, so that you know what you are getting yourself into. Then go to www.mansonsucks.8k.com to get the other side of the story.

370   X-RATING XXX

Drink red bull and vodka.

371   X-RATING XXXX

Get a girl guide leader in a compromising position.

372   X-RATING XXXXX

Shag an ex for old time's sake.

Spin some wax and mix some phat trax...

373

X-RATING XXXX

Sleep on a station platform.

*www3.sympatico.ca/donna.mcsherry/airports.htm offers a great
listing of the facilities of airports and train stations around the world.*

374

X-RATING XXX

Get a job as a club DJ.

375

X-RATING XX

Bench-press 150lbs.

*Remember to:
Load the bar evenly, collars in place and secure. Place your hands evenly
on the bar slightly wider than shoulder-width apart. Make sure your body and
head rest on the bench, legs placed on each side, feet flat on floor. Stabilize
the bar over your upper chest, arms straight, elbows locked, and grip tight.
Lower the bar slowly to your chest in a controlled manner.*

376

X-RATING XXXXX

Shag your girlfriend's older sister
(or her best girlfriend).

377

X-RATING **X**

Own a zoot suit.

378

X-RATING **X**

Eat pie and mash within the sound of Bow Bells.

379

X-RATING **XXXXX**

Hold a poisonous snake (no, not that one).

380

X-RATING **X**

Wear braces.

381

X-RATING **XXX**

Rub thighs with a girl in a split skirt.

382

X-RATING XXXX

Row a girl in a summer dress to a secluded riverside location for a picnic.

Make sure pork is on the menu.

383

X-RATING XXXXX

Drink the whole way down the optics in your favourite pub.

384

X-RATING XXXX

Park up in Lover's Lane for some serious snogging.

385

X-RATING XX

Go on a scooter run to Brighton.

Immortalized in the film Quadrophenia.

386 X-RATING XXXX

Soak your conkers in vinegar.

387 X-RATING XXX

Get it on with a girl with a pierced navel.

www.bodyartdirectories.co.uk will find a body piercing studio for you. Bring your own girl.

388 X-RATING XX

Win first prize in a sweepstake.

389 X-RATING XXX

Belch in front of the vicar before offering him more tea.

390 X-RATING XXXX

Blow a week's wages in the pub.

391 — X-RATING X

Own a hip-flask.

392 — X-RATING XXXXX

Have a sex session with a woman in a choker.

393 — X-RATING X

Eat dim sum on Sunday afternoon in Chinatown.

Dim Sum means 'a little bit of heart'. Dim Sum is Cantonese cuisine coming mainly in the form of steamed and fried dumplings with a wide array of fillings. Many types of dim sum are made with cow's intestine and stomach, pig's blood, chicken feet, and other delicious internal organs.

394 — X-RATING XXXX

Stand a woman up on a cinema date.

395 | X-RATING ——

Own a Nike baseball cap.

396 | X-RATING XX

Torch an amaretto biscuit paper.

Form the paper into a loose cylinder, stand it on one end and set light to the top. It will rise dramatically into the air as it burns.

397 | X-RATING XXXXX

Challenge another driver to a burn-up at the lights.

Put all the chances on your side with the fastest standard production car, a McLaren F1, which can achieve the top speed of 241mph.

398 | X-RATING XXX

Send drinks over to a couple of good looking girls on the other side of the bar.

399 | X-RATING XXXX

Sleep in a ditch.

400

Stuff banknotes into a stripper's g-string.

401

Put a monkey on a horse.

402

Eat a chicken phal.

*'The Phal is, amongst all things culinary, unsurpassed. There is no
hotter sentiment available to the human palette than the explosive
mixture of herbs and spices found in this dish. Finish one and,
"you'll be a man, my son".'*

403

Go muff diving.

X-RATING **XXXX**

Have a kinky spanking session with a woman dressed as a naughty schoolgirl.

X-RATING **X**

Have dinner on the top of the Space Needle in Seattle.

Sky City Restaurant
Space Needle
219 Fourth Avenue North
Seattle
WA 98109, USA.

406

X-RATING **XXXXX**

Shed a tear singing 'Abide With Me' at Wembley Stadium (when it is rebuilt).

"You've been a very naughty girl, haven't you?"

407–416

X-RATING

Quote the following catchphrases in public –

407 'We are the knights who say "Ni"' **XX**

408 'Don't touch the precious things' **XXX**

409 'Don't mention the war' **XX**

410 'Which was nice' **XX**

411 'Is that your final answer?' **XX**

Be aware that, if you come to use this one, the chances are that you will be left to gather the rest of your dignity, get dressed and leave.

412 'You are the weakest link, goodbye' **X**

413 'Whassssuup!' **XX**

414 'Me Tarzan, you Jane' **XXXX**

If you manage to pull this one off, she will swing from your vine all night long.

415 'Where's me washboard?' **X**

416 'You're f**kin' nicked, sunshine' **XXX**

417

X-RATING **XXX**

Go to a club with go-go dancers in a cage.

418

X-RATING **XXXX**

Drive a Lotus 340R.

The Lotus 340R is probably the best-looking, fastest, nimblest, sleekest and sexiest roadster ever created. It only has a 177-horsepower engine but will crank up to around 130mph.

419

X-RATING **XX**

Own a Tivo.

This is the television of the future, and you can record any program digitally. It means you can pause your viewing, go get a beer and come back exactly where you left the show (a bit like pausing an audio tape, but for live TV). You can also replay instantly any portion of the program you are watching without losing any of the show that plays while you are doing so.

420

X-RATING **X**

Have *The Great Escape* theme as your mobile ringing tone.

421
X-RATING **X**

Play the bagpipes.

422
X-RATING **XXXX**

Have sex with the girl next door.

423
X-RATING **XX**

Score a century against your family at beach cricket.

424
X-RATING **XXXXX**

Run the bulls in Pamplona.

The principle is simple: a few bulls are let loose in the streets of Pamplona (Spain) and you have to run in front of them. Pretty dangerous though (a few deaths every year). The high point? See how impressed she will be that you risked your life to show off…

425
X-RATING **XX**

Throw rotten tomatoes in a confined space.

426

X-RATING XXXX

Have a knee-trembler in a dark alley.

427

X-RATING XXX

Buy champagne for a night-club hostess.

428

X-RATING XX

Start… and then abandon a DIY project.

429

X-RATING XXX

Be the first one in and the last one out of the pub.

430

X-RATING XXXX

Play rough with a girl in leopardskin pants.

431

X-RATING XXXXX

Jump into the moshpit at a Metallica concert.

'If it's too loud, you're too old.'

432

X-RATING XXXX

Have sex on a train.

433

X-RATING XXXXX

Drink overproof rum punch.

The Complete Guide to Rum by Edward Hamilton.
www.borders.co.uk

434

X-RATING X

Hang fluffy dice from your rear-view mirror.

435

X-RATING XX

Eat fish 'n' chips on Blackpool promenade.

436

X-RATING XXX

Recite a love poem to someone you fancy.

437

X-RATING XXXX

Have sex in a public toilet (with someone else!).

You should inspect the premises first, if passion leaves you the time, as some very public toilets are riddled with webcams, linked to internet sites.

438

X-RATING XXX

Drop a pen on the floor to look up a woman's skirt.

439

X-RATING XXXX

Have sex in a taxi (you may have to leave a tip).

"My chopper is bigger than yours."

440

X-RATING XXXXX

Have a sword fight.

'In the first place, the quarrels and the bills of the appellant and of the defendant shall be posted in the court before the constable and the marshal. And when they may not prove their cause by witnesses or by any other manner, but must determine their quarrel by strength, the one to prove his intent upon the other and the other in the same manner to defend himself, the constable has power to join the battle as vicar general under God and the king.' Thomas, Duke of Gloucester, Constable under Richard III.

441

X-RATING XXX

Threaten to jump at Lover's Leap.

442

X-RATING XXXX

Unzip a girl in a clinging jumpsuit.

443

X-RATING XXX

Sing a love song to a woman you fancy.

That would have to be 'O Sole Mio', if possible the way Placido Domingo sings it.

444

X-RATING **XXX**

Eat sushi with a geisha girl.

Literally translated, geisha means 'beauty person' or 'person who lives by the arts'. Geishas are trained in music, calligraphy, Sado (tea ceremony), poetry, conversation and social graces as well as at Shamisen (a three-stringed instrument). Sadly not the one-string bass.

445

X-RATING **XXX**

Buy a dodgy CD from the bloke in the pub.

446

X-RATING **XX**

Howl at the moon.

Dogs howl when they are lonely or when they sense great distress in their master's behaviour. Even a change in sleeping habits (brought on by a new girlfriend for instance), will unbalance the 'pack' (the dog's family) and cause the dog to howl.

447

X-RATING **XXXX**

Run a numbers racket.

448

X-RATING XX

Play footsie with a snooty bird at a dinner party.

449

X-RATING XXXX

Get a Danish girl to let you munch her pastry.

450

X-RATING XXXX

Have a bathing beauty scrub your back with a loofah.

The Loofah Gourd (aka Washrag Gourd) is a member of the Cucurbitaceae family, like a cucumber. You can grow it yourself and cut the fruit for your own bathing benefit by buying seeds, or you can take the easier route – your local Boots.

451

X-RATING XXXX

Watch *The Patriot* in an American cinema and cheer as the English slaughter women and children.

452

X-RATING XXX

Buy your girlfriend an ankle bracelet (commonly known as a 'bitch hook') to annoy her mother.

453

X-RATING XXXX

Get lipstick on your collar.

454

X-RATING XXX

Hide a monster love bite.

A love bite is a light subcutaneous oedema brought by vascular stimulation. It occurs when blood is drawn toward the surface of the skin through suction. And yesssss, hiding it or covering it up with makeup is the only way to deal with it while you wait for it to heal.

455

X-RATING XXXXX

Induce a sexual coma.

Coma is a prolonged period of unconsciousness, which is the lack of appreciation of (or reaction to) a stimulus. Coma differs from sleep in that one cannot be aroused from a coma, although someone in a coma can be seen to move and make sounds, but these are only reflex actions.

456

X-RATING XX

Make a sexy librarian blush.

457

X-RATING X

Have a daft CB handle.

458

X-RATING XXXX

Run a pirate radio station.

www.pirateradiouk.com will tell you all you need to know.

459

X-RATING XXX

Be a bog wall graffiti artist.

460

X-RATING X

Watch cricket at the Gabba ground.

The name Gabba is part of Australia's aboriginal heritage – it is short for Woolloongabba, the part of Brisbane, Queensland, where the ground is.

461   X-RATING XXXX

Get your photo in the papers.

Paint yourself red, wear nothing but a rubber band with a cucumber attached to it, stick a satellite dish on your head with gaffer tape and go out for a walk asking people to take you to their leader, with an occasional beep beep or two for good measure.

462   X-RATING XXXXX

Try tantric sex.

Tantra is a form of Hinduism, based on sexuality as a way towards Enlightenment. Following rituals, meditation techniques and Tantra invocations, mantras and yagyas (exercises), you achieve higher states of perception. Sounds good?

463   X-RATING XXXX

Play Adult Consequences.

464   X-RATING XX

Pass the port the wrong way round the table to annoy some old codgers.

465

X-RATING XX

Chew tobacco.

www.skoalbandit.com.

466

X-RATING XXXX

Get sweaty with a Swedish girl.

467

X-RATING XXXXX

Get a Prince Albert piercing.

468

X-RATING X

Grow sideburns.

469

X-RATING XXXX

Play shopping-trolley dodgems in the car park.

470

X-RATING XX

Make the bell ring on a Test Your Strength stall at a fairground.

471

X-RATING XXXX

Waterski off the back of a speedboat.

Learn with TV Ski Ltd
Sunneymeads Lake
Horton Road
Datchet
Berkshire SL3 9HY.

472

X-RATING X

Wear a white tuxedo.

473

X-RATING X

Watch international rugby at Twickenham, Murrayfield, Cardiff, Dublin, Paris and Rome.

www.railchoice.co.uk.

The perfect addition to a white tux – arm candy.

474

X-RATING **XXX**

Puke on the steps of your least favourite
football club.

475

X-RATING **XXXX**

Get an Australian girl to blow on your didgeridoo.

476

X-RATING **XXX**

Invite a girl upstairs to 'see your etchings'.

477

X-RATING **XXXXX**

Have a sex session with a woman in handcuffs.

478

X-RATING **XX**

Shave your legs.

*You have a choice of various methods: plucking, depilatory creams,
sugaring, waxing, threading… Visiting your girlfriend's regular
beauty salon with her is not one of them though.*

479

X-RATING X

Eat fresh bagels as the day dawns on Sunday.

Why do seagulls fly over the sea?
Because if they flew over the bay they'd be bagels.

480

X-RATING XXXXX

Go jaywalking.

481

X-RATING XX

Throw 501 in 9 darts, straight in and close on a double.

482

X-RATING XXXX

Finish a kebab the next morning.

Indigestion, or to give it its proper name, dyspepsia, has various causes.
Amongst them is, of course, bad eating habits. A shot of bicarbonate
of soda should make you feel better.

483

X-RATING XXX

Carve your name on a tree.

484

X-RATING **XX**

Beat the Germans to the pool while on holiday in the Mediterranean.

485

X-RATING **XXX**

Twang the g-string of a girl in hipsters.

A well-tuned g-string, when plucked, should give a perfect A.

486

X-RATING **XXX**

Lay a monster log around the side of the toilet bowl.

A diet of freshly-cooked vegetables, high fibre cereals and brown bread is the best recipe for huge dumps.

487

X-RATING **XXX**

Play horsey-horsey with a country girl.

488

X-RATING **XXXX**

Umpire a game of women's beach volleyball.

489

X-RATING **X**

Score a hole-in-one at golf.

490

X-RATING **XXXX**

Do a wheelie on a motorbike.

This is not as difficult as it sounds. All you need to do is depress the clutch, rev up and release quickly. Remember though that a fracture of the coccyx is very painful and extremely uncomfortable (and extremely silly too).

491

X-RATING **XXXX**

Make love on black satin sheets.

Actually, this is not such a good idea: while satin sheets undoubtedly look good, when wet they are as slippery as a soggy banana.

492

X-RATING **XXX**

Crash the night on a relative stranger's sofa.

493

X-RATING **X**

Buy a Tommy Hilfiger jacket.

494
X-RATING X

Customize a Capri.

www.mistral.co.uk/pipes/fccoc.html.

495
X-RATING XXX

Toke on a one-hit bong.

496
X-RATING X

Win a five-a-side football tournament.

497
X-RATING X

Roll down the Dune de Pilar in France.

The largest sand dune in Europe, 1.7 miles long and 1,200 feet wide.
Climbing the 190 steps to the top is knackering, but the view is unforgettable.

498
X-RATING XX

Place a winning spread bet.

499

X-RATING X

Whisper sweet nothings to a friend in the
St Paul's Cathedral gallery.

Nearest Underground station: St Paul's: 5 minutes' walk from the Cathedral.

500

X-RATING X

Dance with your cat.

The only dance you can do with a cat is the swing.

501

X-RATING XXX

Win an arm-wrestling championship.

502

X-RATING XXXXX

Explore ten erogenous zones.

*The largest sensory organ for both men and women is the skin itself,
especially the inner thigh area, the neck, the breasts and nipples, and the
perineum. Other erogenous zones include the eyelids, the ears, and
the shoulders, the buttocks, the feet and, of course, the genitals.*

Mating ritals of Modern Men, No. 4:
displaying one's assets.

503

Moon out of a coach window to relieve the
tedium of a long journey.

Alternatively, cut out centrefolds of Playboy *or page 3s prior to the trip
and saliva-stick them on the coach windows for all the world to see.*

504

X-RATING **XXX**

Lend a girlfriend one of your shirts to wear for
breakfast at your place.

505

X-RATING **XXXX**

Rub noses with a girl from a cold climate.

506

X-RATING **XX**

Drive an open-topped sports car with a gorgeous
blonde in the passenger seat.

507
X-RATING XXXX

Bivouac in the woods in Transylvania.

508
X-RATING XX

Clear the pool table from the break.

509
X-RATING X

Ride a scooter to the Isle of Man.

510
X-RATING XXXXX

Have a sex session with a woman in a blindfold.

511
X-RATING XXXXX

Own a Mont Blanc fountain pen.

The Mont Blanc is a monster pen, the ultimate writing toy... at a price: 'Le Doue Royal Hommage a Wolfgang Amadeus' has an 18-carat gold body, a cap set with 1,270 diamonds, a mother of pearl logo and a handcrafted 18-carat gold nib inlaid with platinium.

See the seven wonders of the Ancient World

512 The Great Pyramid at Giza. **X**

'Man fears Time, yet Time fears the Pyramids'
(Arab proverb).

513 The Hanging Gardens of Babylon. **X**

514 The Statue of Zeus at Olympia. **X**

515 The Temple of Artemis **X**
at Ephesus.

This temple was acclaimed as the most beautiful
structure on Earth, dedicated to the goddess
Artemis, or Diana, goddess of hunting and nature.

516 The Mausoleum at Halicarnassus **X**
(present-day Bodrum).

517 The Lighthouse of Alexandria. **X**

The only one of the seven wonders to actually have
a practical purpose, the Lighthouse of Alexandria
was built on the island of Pharos by Ptolemy Soter
around 290 BC. It had a mirror whose reflection
could be seen more than 35 miles away.

518 The Colossus of Rhodes. **X**

An enormous statue dedicated to the Greek god
Helios, god of the sun, in the harbour town of Rhodes.
It was so big (about 100ft high) that boats sailed
underneath it. It took 12 years to build (finished
282 BC) and was destroyed at the knees after
an earthquake hit the city 56 years later.

519

X-RATING X

Own a Swiss army knife.

Invented in 1891 by Master Cutter Karl Elsener, the 'Offiziermesser' was nicknamed 'Swiss army knife' by GIs during World War II because they couldn't pronounce its original name.

520

X-RATING XXX

Drink Bloody Marys to ease a hangover.

The Bloody Mary cocktail was invented by Fernand Petiot, an American bartender at Harry's New York Bar in Paris, by mixing equal amounts of tomato juice and vodka. It was called Bloody Mary because it reminded his boss of the Bucket of Blood Club in Chicago, and of a girl he knew there named Mary. Petiot later on spiced it up with black pepper, cayenne pepper, Worcestershire sauce, lemon and Tabasco.

521

X-RATING XXXX

Be invited in for a nibble by a bored housewife.

522

X-RATING XXXX

Smoke 40 fags in a day.

523
X-RATING XXXXX

Make love to a woman dressed only in high heels and pearls (her, not you).

524
X-RATING XXXX

Get hand relief from a nail technician.

525
X-RATING XX

Own a pinkie ring.

526
X-RATING XXXX

Strike sparks off your blakies from a motorbike.

527
X-RATING XX

Be mistaken for a celebrity.

528

X-RATING ——

✳ Gel your hair.

529

X-RATING XXXXX

Wear Issey Miyake Pour Homme.

Issey Miyake comes out top of the Loaded *best men's perfume list year after year: a true fanny-magnet. Get it from:*
Issey Miyake Boutiques
992 Madison Avenue
New York
NY, USA.

530

X-RATING XX

Cut down a tree with a chainsaw.

531

X-RATING XXXXX

Study a martial art.

Learn effective self-defence techniques, zazen meditation and body manipulation for well-being and pain relief.
Shorinji Kempo in London:
www.abbeydojo.co.uk.

Face protection is essential when
wielding a large chopper.

532 | X-RATING X

See the Northern Lights.

Also known as Auroras Borealis, *these are flows of solar winds, entering the ionosphere and hitting gasses. They produce spectacular colour shifts. In the Antarctic region they are called* Aurora Australis, *or Southern Lights.*

533–542 | X-RATING

See the top ten sick movies –

533   *Happiness* (Todd Solondz, 1998)*o   XXXXX

Plain old unpleasant.

534   *Padre Padrone* (Paolo Taviani & Vittorio Taviani, 1977)   XXXXX

You'll never eat lamb again.

535   *Natural Born Killers* (Oliver Stone, 1994)   XXX

Still banned on video.

536   *Romance* (Catherine Breillat, 1999)*   XXXXX

Nasty French bird's boyfriend won't do the business. This could have fitted into the porn film list.

537   *Salo*, or *120 Days of Sodom* (Pier Paolo Pasolini, 1975)*   XXXXX

Banned in the UK for decades: it's nasty.

538 *From Dusk till Dawn*   **XXXX**
 (Robert Rodriguez, 1995)*o

Weird shit.

539 *La Grande Bouffe* (*Blow-out*)   **XXXXX**
(Marco Ferreri, 1973)*o

Fat French blokes eat and shag themselves to death:
the reason arty movies attract the dirty raincoat brigade.

540 *Henry – Portrait of a Serial Killer*   **XXXXX**
(John McNaughton, 1990)*o

Very nasty.

541 *Man Bites Dog* (Rémy Belvaux,   **XXXXX**
André Bonzel, Benoît Poelvoorde, 1992)*o

Another story of a serial killer, but this time
it's funny – black humour.

542 *Society* (Brian Wuzna 1989)*o   **XXXX**

Just plain sick.

* DVD   o VHS

---

543   X-RATING **XXXXX**

Get an Italian girl to pummel your salami.

544   X-RATING **XX**

Charter a jet to fly from London to the Isle of Wight.

545
X-RATING XX

Visit the Cannes Film Festival.

'The spirit of the Cannes Film Festival is one of friendship and universal cooperation. Its aim is to reveal and focus attention on works of quality in order to contribute to the progress of the motion picture arts and to encourage the development of the film industry throughout the world.' (Submission rules)

546
X-RATING XXX

Drive from Land's End to John O'Groats without stopping.

547
X-RATING XXXXX

Lie on a bed of nails.

When you lie on a bed of nails, your weight is distributed over hundreds of nails, so each area supports a fraction of your weight. Visit www.pitt.edu/~dwilley/nailbed.html to build your own bed of nails.

548
X-RATING XX

Have a coffee in a revolving restaurant on a mountain in the Alps.

549

X-RATING X

Go all the way round the Circle Line on the London Underground.

Doing it once only should suffice.

550

X-RATING XXX

Ask a French woman if she's ever been to Africa.

551

X-RATING XXXX

Urinate off the Petronas Towers in Malaysia.

The tallest towers in the world are 1,400 feet tall.
They are situated in Kuala Lumpur, Malaysia.

552

X-RATING X

Bet on a white Christmas.

553

X-RATING XXXX

Email a picture of yourself in the buff to a woman you just met.

554 X-RATING XX

Go back to your first school in a Ferrari and shout at the teachers.

555 X-RATING XXXXX

Hotwire a car.

The Worst-Case Scenario Survival Handbook *by Joshua Piven and David Borgenicht covers just this eventuality.*

556 X-RATING XXXX

Contest the annual Paris–Dakar race.

It will cost you up to 73,000FF to register, plus 50,000FF for ground assistance and an optional 40,000FF for air assistance, payable to Banque Nationale de Paris 16, Boulevard des Italiens 75009 Paris, France.

557 X-RATING X

Get a fake tan.

A full size sunbed should cost you around £900 from Index. They also do a face tan lamp for around £55.

558

X-RATING XX

Follow a juicy law case from the public gallery.

559

X-RATING XXX

Tango with a woman with a rose between her teeth.

560

X-RATING XX

Send some Spitfire beer to a German friend.

'Downed all over Kent, Just like the Luftwaffe'
www.shepherd-neame.co.uk.

561

X-RATING XXXX

Have a sex session with a woman with a feather boa.

First Night will rent you anything from a feather boa to a
maid's apron or a Cat Woman outfit.
Tel: 01908 262250.

562

X-RATING XXX

Drive a car around the streets of San Francisco.

563   X-RATING **XXXXX**

Visit the Bois de Boulogne in Paris.

The hot spot of Paris, to be visited at night. Expect to be solicited by female and male prostitutes as well as transvestites of both sexes.

564   X-RATING **XXX**

Break planks of wood in a Tae Kwon Do class.

565   X-RATING **XXXXX**

Have a *Nine-and-a-half-weeks*-style food/sex session.

566   X-RATING **XXX**

Ride a Harley–Davidson.

A 1,445cc, twin cam 88 vibration solation-mounted engine, 5 gear, 2-tone suede green and black Tourer Road King can be yours for around £12,800.

567   X-RATING **XXX**

Get into a fight with one of your mates.

568

X-RATING X

Have a swing at playing baseball.

If you want to understand such arcane terms as tags, fly ball, fair ball, infielder and battery, go to www.eteamz.com/baseball.

569

X-RATING X

Attend the Lisdoonvarna Rock Festival.

Lisdoonvarna is in County Clare, Republic of Ireland.

570

X-RATING XXXX

Have a dirty weekend in the country.

571

X-RATING XX

Visit the Edinburgh festival.

Annually, from August to September
Edinburgh International Festival
The Hub
Castlehill
Edinburgh EH1 2NE.

Wear your heart on your sleeve with a tattoo.

572

Have a tattoo.

573

Go to a Star Trek convention dressed as Spock.

You'll probably find some information on the Internet for this one…

574

See and be seen at Glorious Goodwood.

Goodwood Racecourse
Goodwood
West Sussex
Tel: 01243 755022
www.gloriousgoodwood.co.uk

575

Spend a weekend to remember in Tijuana –
the Happiest Place on Earth.

Tijuana is one of the most visited places on the planet, with 36 million
people passing through it every year. It is the border town between the
USA and Mexico, thriving on gambling, greyhound racing, bullfighting
and sex, although less now as the city has been cleaned up.

576 X-RATING **X**

Be in Hollywood for the Oscars™ ceremony.

577 X-RATING ——

Scan your own purchases on the laser-operated tills at Sainsbury's.

578 X-RATING **X**

Look up your name on the Internet.

579 X-RATING **X**

Get a Premiership footballer's autograph.

If you can't face queuing and lying that it's for your little brother, try http://auctions.excite.co.uk or www.ebay.com.

580 X-RATING **XXXX**

Have sex in a lift.

581

X-RATING X

Visit Monument Valley.

With its strong Navajo Indian culture, Monument Valley is magic, full of impressive monoliths of reddish rock, dessert sandstorms and incredible views. Monument Valley Tribal Park, open May–September daily 07:00–19:00; October–April daily 08:00–17:00, $2.50 entrance fee.

582

X-RATING XXX

Go on a wilderness training weekend.

Bob Bull
15 Cross Lanes
Pill
North Somerset
BS20 0JQ
Tel: 01275 375407.

583

X-RATING X

Go to a show at the Paris Opéra.

Palais Garnier
Place de l'Opéra
Paris
France
Metro: Opéra

584

X-RATING **X**

Have a row in a coxless pairs boat.

585

X-RATING **XXXX**

Sit in the away fans' end for a whole football match.

586

X-RATING **XXX**

Dress as a vicar for an evening down the pub.

587

X-RATING **XXXX**

Get an Irish colleen to stroke your shillelagh.

588

X-RATING **XXXX**

Put clingfilm over a toilet seat.

589

X-RATING XXX

Slag off your least favourite celebrity in person.

590

X-RATING XX

Take the night train from Mombasa to Nairobi.

*Departure 19.00, arrival 08.40. First, second and third class available.
Restaurant on board (attend the second dinner sitting).
Fare: 2,750.00 Ksh (around £25).*

591

X-RATING X

Visit a rainforest.

That is, if there is still one left by the time you marry. Try Ecuador or Peru.

592

X-RATING XXX

Pee in a swimming pool.

*However, this will not remain unseen in most cases because the colour of
your urine will certainly not match the colour of the pool water. Some chemicals
found in pools also react to urine, making the contrast brighter… You might find
yourself floating in an embarrassing pool of glowing yellow water.*

593 X-RATING XXX

Take a Gameboy to a work meeting – and play it.

594 X-RATING XXXX

Work as a lifeguard on a nude beach.

595 X-RATING X

See a football match at the Maracana stadium.

Maracana stadium is one of the world's largest. It was built in Rio de Janeiro for the World Cup in 1950.

596 X-RATING XXX

Go to Easter Island.

1,200 years ago some adventurers discovered Easter Island and colonized it. They soon started carving giant faces, or 'moai', in the volcanic rock, before disappearing. After years and years of research, this still remains one of the most mysterious places on Earth.

597 X-RATING XXXX

Read a porno mag with your girlfriend.

598

X-RATING X

Buy an MP3 player.

Diamond Rio 600 MP3 player, around £150 from Dixons,
or choose a non-portable version, such as the Samsung
MMN75M MP3 Hi-Fi system for around £350.

599

X-RATING XXX

Ask a Turkish woman for a kebab.

600

X-RATING XX

Drive a Hummer.

It is flat, low, slowish (maximum 90mph), so why would you want to drive one?
Ah well, yes but they have a button to inflate or deflate tyres on the fly, loops
for military airlift on the bonnet, and they can cross up to 3 feet of water...
not to mention how cool they look.

601

X-RATING XX

Sing 'The Hills Are Alive' with a Swiss
miss in the Alps.

602
X-RATING XX

Ask a woman if she's a part-time model.

603
X-RATING XXX

Swim naked in a Scottish loch.

That would have to be Loch Lomond: misty, mysterious and so romantic.
Follow the A82 North from Glasgow to the local tourist office
(Open April–October, various hours, always after 10.00 am).
Tel: 01389 753533.

604
X-RATING XXXXX

Ask your girlfriend to have a 'W' tattooed on each bum cheek.

It may not look like much, but when she bends over naked: wow!

605
X-RATING XX

Get a supermodel's autograph.

606

X-RATING XXX

Pass an orange from under your chin to under the chin of a woman in a halter top – without using hands.

607

X-RATING XX

Fly on Concorde.

The summit in terms of comfort and speed
(London–New York in three hours 50 minutes).

608

X-RATING XXX

Abseil down one of the huge Hollywood letters.

The mother of all signs was built in 1923 on the side of Mt Cahuenga in
Los Angeles, California. It first spelled 'Hollywoodland' and was conceived
as an ad stunt by a real estate company.

609

X-RATING XX

Be on a TV quiz show.

610

X-RATING **XX**

Go weight training on Muscle Beach.

Muscle Beach is Part of the City of Los Angeles Department of Recreation and Parks. It is where muscular, tanned and healthy-looking men come to train.

611

X-RATING **XXXX**

Have a dump in a hole in a golf course.

612

X-RATING **XXXXX**

Have sex on the back seat of a Mini.

613

X-RATING **X**

Go to the foothills of Everest.

Here is your itinerary for around eight days of solid trekking – after you've landed in Nepal: Lukla, Namche (11,385ft), Tengboche, Pangboche, Pheriche (14,025ft), Lobuche (16,269ft), Gorak Shep (17,094), Kala Pattar, Everest Base Camp. Dress Warmly and beware of AMS (Acute Mountain Sickness).

"Squeeze up – there's room for just one more!"

614

X-RATING **XXXX**

Spend a week partying in Goa.

615

X-RATING **X**

Own a minidisc player.

The Sony MZR900L jogproof recordable personal minidisc player with longplay does look funky.

616

X-RATING **XXX**

Ask seven different women you've never met before for a date every day for a week.

617

X-RATING **XX**

Sit in the back row of a cinema and throw popcorn at people in front of you until you get thrown out.

618

X-RATING **XXXX**

See a show at Raymond's Revue Bar, Soho.

619

X-RATING **X**

Get on a radio phone-in.

620

X-RATING **XXXXX**

Go bungee jumping.

BERSA (British Elastic Rope Sports Association)
33A Canal Street
Oxford
OX2 6BQ
Tel: 01865 311179.

621

X-RATING **XXXXX**

Have sex in a packed crowd at a concert
(not a Pavarotti concert).

622

X-RATING **XX**

Enter a Strongman contest.

Here's what you'll have to do if you want to beat Janni Virtannen, sacred
Strongman of the Year in 2000:
Log lift for maximum weight
Car pull (such as a Humvee over 400yds)
Tyre Flip: 45ft
Loading Race: 154lbs keg, 220lbs sack, 231lbs keg, 242lbs log, 286lbs stone.

623
X-RATING XXXXX

Get a mademoiselle to bite your baguette.

624
X-RATING X

Have your fortune told.

You have a choice of methods here: astrology, verses, numerology, handology, cards, wigan horoscope… The best of all could be rune stone casting, available at:
Internetticom
246 Church Road
Thundersley
Benfleet
Essex SS7 4PL
Tel: 01268 565173.

625
X-RATING XXXX

Have a full-body massage.

626
X-RATING X

Own a digital camera.

The Olympus D 490Z boasts 2.11 million pixels, 2x digital zoom and a motion picture mode, for a mere £349.

627

Get a letter published in an agony aunt column.

628

Snog a woman over 50.

629

Own a pocket-PC.

Get yourself a Hewlett-Packard Jordana 545, compatible with PC and Macintosh, 133mhz processor, 16mb memory, infrared and USB ports.

630

Serenade a woman from beneath her bedroom window.

You could also let the matters in the capable hands of Susan Heaton-Wright (soprano) and Neil Simon (classical guitar), forming the duo Serenata. Email david@wedding-services.demon.co.uk for more details and a demo pack.

631   X-RATING **XX**

Take a female student to see an arty-farty
French movie.

Not La Grande Bouffe
Take her to the Ciné Lumière, the cinema at the French Institute
17 Queensberry Place
London SW7 2DT.

632   X-RATING **XXX**

Jog across Dartmoor.

633   X-RATING **XX**

Go 'commando' for a day (no underwear).

634   X-RATING **XX**

Ask for 'a long sloe screw against the wall'
in a cocktail bar.

635

X-RATING XX

Write a steamy love letter and send it to your prospective in-laws by 'accident'.

636

X-RATING XXX

See a witch-doctor in Haiti.

637

X-RATING X

Drink a stein of lager at the Munich Beer Festival.

The Oktoberfest in Munich, Germany, draws around 7 million visitors who consume 5 million kegs of beer, 700,000 fried chicken legs, 400,000 pairs of bratwurst (pork sausages) and pee in 1,440 toilets. The most famous attraction might not be the beer though, but the waitresses, who are between 18 and 80.

638

X-RATING XXX

Visit the Taj Mahal.

The Indian classical poet Tagore called it a 'tear on the face of eternity'. It was built between 1635 and 1653 by Shah Jahan in loving memory of his departed wife Mumtaz Mahal.

639
X-RATING XXX

Go clubbing in Ayia Napa.

You will be spoiled for choice, with places such as Grease Disco, Starsky and Hutch Club, Minos Pub, Ice Ku… A villa for 5 in Nissi Beach, Cyprus, will cost you around £490 for a week in August. Contact:
Cyprus Villa
PO Box 40218
Larnaca
Cyprus.

640
X-RATING XXXXX

Have anonymous email sex with a stranger.

641
X-RATING X

 Own a DVD player with full surround sound.

Don't forget to get multi-region if you want to take advantage of cheap US imports.

642
X-RATING XXXX

Go parachuting with the marines.

643

X-RATING XX

Have a beery barbie on Bondi Beach.

First you need to go to Sydney, then take the 380, 382 or L82 bus from Circular Quay to either North Bondi, Dover Heights or Bondi Beach.

644

X-RATING XXXXX

Do a ski jump.

645

X-RATING X

Own a 6-cell Maglite.

Get one from:
The Toolshed
46 The Lanes
Meadowhall
Sheffield
South Yorkshire
Tel: 0114 256 9661.

646

X-RATING XXX

Follow the British Lions on a rugby tour.

Let's do the Time Warp again…

647

X-RATING XXX

Dress up for a showing of the *Rocky Horror Picture Show*.

'Give yourself over to absolute pleasure. Swim the warm waters of sins of the flesh – erotic nightmares beyond any measure, and sensual daydreams to treasure forever. Can't you just see it? Don't dream it, be it.'

648

X-RATING X

Have an all-night Tekken session on a Playstation 2.

In the all-out battle for game console domination between Playstation2, Dreamcast and the Microsoft xBox, the PS2 from Sony, with Dolby Digital Sound and graphic synthesiser, seems to be the one to buy, despite its pricetag.

649

X-RATING X

Own a GPS.

Global Positioning Sytems, or GPS, will let you know where you are at all time. Install an Ericsson MC218 & Palmtop GPS with Street Planner Millennium in your car, a Garmin GBR21 in your boat, or strap a Casio Protek GPS 2watch around your wrist... for a price. www.uk2.21store.com.

650–659   X-RATING

Own ten classic CDs –

650   *Astral Weeks* – Van Morrison   **XX**

651   *Led Zep IV* – Led Zepplin   **XXXX**

652   *Screamadelica* – Primal Scream   **XX**

653   *The Clash* – The Clash   **XXXX**

654   *What's The Story*   **XXX**
       (Morning Glory) – Oasis

655   *Check Your Head* –   **XXX**
       the Beastie Boys

656   *Live Cream* – Cream   **XXXX**

657   *Never Mind the Bollocks* –   **XXXXX**
       the Sex Pistols

658   *Enema of the State* – Blink 182   **XXX**

659   *Leftfield* – Leftfield   **XXX**

660

X-RATING XX

Attend a Super Bowl party in the U.S.

The game is played on the fourth or fifth Sunday in January.

661

X-RATING XXXX

Do a stunt bicycle jump into a river.

662

X-RATING XXX

Go to a post-pub, late-night showing of *The Exorcist*.

663

X-RATING X

Book a table at Ronnie Scott's, Soho.

47 Frith Street
Soho
London W1D 4HT
Tel: 020 7439 0747.

664
X-RATING XX

Dance salsa at Bar Rumba, London.

36 Shaftesbury Avenue
London W1D 7EP
Tel: 020 7287 2715.

665
X-RATING X

Pretend to be a waxwork at Madame Tussauds.

Marylebone Road
London NW1 5LR
Nearest Underground: Baker Street, (Bakerloo, Circle, Jubilee,
Metropolitan, and Hammersmith & City Lines – two minutes' walk).

666
X-RATING X

Own and grow some Sea Monkeys.

If you feel all alone and need a friend in a hurry, open a packet of sea monkeys
and place in a container of water. These brine shrimps actually live in a kind of
suspended animation in their eggs, waiting for the proper environment to arise
to grow and thrive. Get your starter kit from www.amazon.com.

667
X-RATING XXX

Drive an HGV.

668   X-RATING **XXXX**

Go to a strip club.

669   X-RATING **XXX**

Eat a hash cake before attending a showing of your favourite Monty Python movie.

670   X-RATING **X**

Own an AppleMac PowerCube.

Apple strikes again, after having revolutionized the computer industry with the iMac, by producing a silent integrated system (no noisy cooling fan) that looks absolutely gorgeous. Check it out on www.apple.com.

671   X-RATING **X**

Own a LCD flatscreen television.

672

X-RATING **XXXXX**

Have sex with a woman in uniform.

673

X-RATING ———

Complete a Panini sticker collection.

674

X-RATING **X**

Own a portable MP3 player-mobile phone.

675

X-RATING **X**

Climb Vesuvius in Naples.

Vesuvius was the volcano that caused the tragedy of Pompei (killing 20,000 people with a blast of toxic gas travelling at 320mph and then burying them alive). Today, researchers reckon there could be another eruption in the next ten years. But they are not sure...

676 | **X-RATING XX**

Take your girlfriend to a football match.

677 | **X-RATING XX**

Doctor photographs to make a picture of you goosing Naomi Campbell.

678 | **X-RATING XXX**

Drive a train.

679 | **X-RATING XXXX**

See the wild gorillas in Uganda.

Footprint Adventures
5 Malham Drive
Lincoln LN6 0XD
Tel: 01522 804929.

680

X-RATING **XXXX**

Meet a woman through small ads.

681

X-RATING **X**

Own a digital video camera.

682

X-RATING **XXXX**

Persuade a cheerleader to do the splits for you.

683

X-RATING **XXXXX**

Be covered in chocolate and have women lick it off.

You can now even find body chocolate in mainstream places such as BHS, for around £5 a jar.

"What was it they call the Oregon State University team? Oh, yes, the Beavers."

684

X-RATING **XX**

Drink a 'depth charge'.

Any spirit in a shot glass, dropped into a pint of beer or lager.
The shot glass's weight causes an interesting ripple effect.
The drink is then downed, normally in one.

685

X-RATING **X**

Write a letter to your MP.

686

X-RATING **X**

Watch all the *Star Wars* movies back-to-back.

Episode 1:The Phantom Menace
Star Wars
The Empire Strikes Back
Return of the Jedi

687

X-RATING **X**

Eat sushi in Tokyo.

688 X-RATING X

See a film in every screen of a multiplex cinema on the same day/weekend.

689 X-RATING XXX

Have a bath with a Cleopatra-look-alike in asses' milk.

Brigitte Bardot did it in Les Week-ends de Neron, *when she asked for the starch and water she was bathing in to be swapped for real milk. Under the projector's heat the milk turned to yoghurt. You have been warned.*

690 X-RATING XX

Attend a showing of *Reservoir Dogs* with the lads dressed in black suits, ties and shades.

691 X-RATING X

Own an Audi TT convertible.

692

X-RATING **XX**

Perform an act on the street at Covent Garden.

Stripping off and running down the street chasing pigeons will not be considered an act by the Metropolitan Police.

693

X-RATING **X**

Win a pub quiz.

694

X-RATING **X**

Visit Rorke's Drift in South Africa.

On January 22, 1879, the whole 1,700 men of a British colonial force were defeated by Zulu warriors. Later in the evening, a bunch of veterans and sick successfully defended a field hospital across from the site of the earlier disaster.

695

X-RATING **XXXXX**

Referee a football match on Hackney Marshes.

696 X-RATING **X**

Smoke a pipe.

697 X-RATING **XX**

Drink the milk from a freshly-cut coconut on a
South Seas beach.

698 X-RATING **XXX**

Fly through the Bermuda Triangle.

*This is the region between Bermuda, Miami, Florida and San Juan, Puerto Rico.
It is famous for the unnatural number of planes, tankers and ships of all shapes
that have disappeared there. Some of the weirdest theories involve Atlantis,
UFOs stealing earthlings, time warp spots and Prehistoric super-civilizations.*

699 X-RATING **XXXX**

Spend a week on a desert island with your Girl Friday.

700   X-RATING ——

Take a ferry 'cross the Mersey.

701   X-RATING **XXX**

Buy something in a Moroccan Souk.

702   X-RATING **XXX**

Travel overland from London to Capetown.

703   X-RATING **XXX**

Join a public protest against the government/taxation/ hunting/banning of hunting.

704   X-RATING **XXX**

Dye your hair grey and go to Stringfellows.

16–19 Upper St Martin's Lane
Covent Garden
London WC2.

705

Have a cast made of your erect penis.

www.adultsextoysuk.co.uk to the rescue! Mould-a-willy kit to make a perfect replica of your organ and a rubber vibrator out of it in a couple of evenings. Only £19.99.

706

Own a Nakamichi cassette player.

707

Climb to the top of the Statue of Liberty, New York

She was a gift from 'the French people to the American people' by master sculptor Frederic-Auguste Bartholdi, who had originally thought her to be a new Wonder of the World to mark Egypt's Suez Canal. There are ferries to Ellis Island from Battery Park every 30–45 minutes.

708

Pot a 147 break at a snooker table.

709
X-RATING **XX**

Discuss existentialism on the banks of the Seine.

710
X-RATING **XXX**

Spoon a ladle of water on the hot coals
in a mixed sauna.

711
X-RATING **XXX**

Travel up the Amazon.

Galapagos Adventure Tours will take you there and back
79 Maltings Place
169 Tower Bridge Road
London SE1 3LJ.
Tel: 020 7407 1478.

712
X-RATING **X**

Direct the traffic at an open air car park.

713

X-RATING **XXXX**

Try to pull a woman in a gay bar.

714

X-RATING **XXX**

Fart loudly in church.

715

X-RATING **XX**

Get a turbo fitted to your car.

716

X-RATING **XX**

Attend a World Cup Final.

717

X-RATING **XXXXX**

Spend a whole weekend in bed.

"Looks like we're stuck here together
for a two-week train ride."

718

X-RATING X

Own an AppleMac Titanium laptop.

Just one inch thick and with a body made of commercially pure titanium, the Apple Titanium PowerBook G4 is a beast of design and technology: a 500mhz processor hooked to a Velocity Engine (making it 30% faster than a PC counterpart), a DVD Rom drive, an S-video output slot, USB, Firewire and 10/1,000 Base-T Ethernet card.

719

X-RATING XXX

Fire a shotgun at a rifle range.

720

X-RATING XXX

Have a snowball fight in Iceland with a Björk look-alike.

721

X-RATING XXXX

Travel on the Orient Express.

A trip on the famous Venice Simplon-Orient-Express, London–Paris–Venice will cost you around £1,500. And no, at that price, you do not get to murder somebody.

722 X-RATING **X**

Ride to the top of the Eiffel Tower in Paris.

The tower is made of 18,000 steel pieces, 2,500,000 rivets and requires 50 tons of paint every 7 years. You can take the stairs up to the second floor, but need to take the lift to go higher and reach the 300m mark.

723 X-RATING **XX**

Drive a '57 Chevy.

www.chevroleteurope.com will introduce you to the new models from Chevrolet, while www.american-auto-club.co.uk will offer you loads of info about your favourite American cars.

724 X-RATING **X**

Give a tramp a £20 note.

725 X-RATING **XXXX**

Have a boxing sparring session with a professional.

726

X-RATING **X**

Take a ride in a submarine.

727

X-RATING **XX**

Smoke Sobranie Black Russian cigarettes.

McGahey The Tobacconist
245 High Street
Exeter
Devon EX4 3NZ.
Tel: 01392 496111.

728

X-RATING **XX**

Have your back done by a chiropractor.

Daniel David Palmer pioneered chiropractics in 1895 (he was
jailed one year later for practising without a medical licence).
www.chiropractic.co.uk has an online directory.

729

X-RATING **XX**

Visit Mexico on Day of the Dead.

Dating back to a ritual taking place in the Aztec month of Miccailhuitontli, presided by the goddess Mictecacihuatl (Lady of the Dead) and dedicated to children and the dead, this is the Mexican holiday, a time when they remember their dead but also celebrate the continuity of life. Mexican people will go and visit their relatives' graves and picnic there, and also eat 'pan de muerto' or 'bread of the dead' that has a plastic luck-bringing skeleton hidden inside it.

730

X-RATING **XXXXX**

Drink Absinthe.

Absinthe was enjoyed by intellectuals and artists such as Beaudelaire, van Gogh and Verlaine in Paris at the turn of the century for its aphrodisiac and hallucinogenic virtues. Its production is still banned in most European countries as its main ingredient, wormwood, is considered toxic.

731

X-RATING **XX**

Have your nails done by a beautician.

732

X-RATING **X**

Spend a weekend on the sofa watching football.

See the top ten horror movies –

733	*Day of the Dead* (1985)*o	**XXXX**
734	*The Blair Witch Project* (1999)*o	**XXXX**
735	*The Devils* (1970)*o	**XXX**
736	*The Sixth Sense* (1999)*o	**XXX**
737	*Motel Hell* (1980)o	**XXX**
738	*Body Parts* (1991)*o	**XXXX**
739	*The Texas Chainsaw Massacre* (1974)*o	**XXXXX**
740	*The Driller Killer* (1979)*o	**XXXXX**
741	*Demons* (1985)*o	**XXXX**
742	*Repulsion* (1965)o	**XXXXX**

* DVD　　o VHS

743

X-RATING **XX**

Buy a scooter in Milan and ride it back to England.

744

X-RATING **X**

Get a leased line for your internet connection.

A 512mb connection for £9,000 a year, available from:
ewNet Ltd.
Cams Hall Estate
Fareham
Hampshire PO16 8UT.

745

X-RATING **X**

Own a Dukla Prague away kit.

746

X-RATING **XX**

Have a 'Frank Zappa' all-night fancy dress party.

747

X-RATING XX

Wear a gorilla suit to work.

748

X-RATING X

Walk the length of Hadrian's Wall.

Northumberland County Council
County Hall
Morpeth
Northumberland NE61 2EF.

749

X-RATING X

Have your flat/house spring cleaned by professionals.

750

X-RATING XXXX

Employ a female escort to accompany you
for a business meal.

Sirens models and companions: www.sirens-escorts.com.

751

X-RATING XXX

Be a sperm donor.

London Fertility Centre
Cozens House
112A Harley Street
London W1N 1AF
Tel: 020 7224 0707.

752

X-RATING XXX

Pretend to be a model scout to take pictures
of women.

753

X-RATING XXXXX

Play blackjack in a Vegas casino.

www.luxor.com
Luxor Resort and Casino
3900 Las Vegas Blvd
Las Vegas
NV 89119
USA.

754

X-RATING XX

Belch a whole song.

Luck be your ladies tonight.

755

X-RATING X

Own a pair of Technics decks.

Treat yourself to a pair of SL-1200M3D Direct-Drive turntables.
www.technics.co.uk.

756

X-RATING X

Own a set of walkie-talkies.

RadioShack 14-Channel FRS 2-Way Personal Radio: £69.99.

757

X-RATING XXX

Chat up a woman on a bus.

758

X-RATING XXXX

Drive a Subaru on a skid pan.

759

X-RATING XX

Climb a tree.

760

X-RATING XXXXX

Enter the Isle of Man TT race.

Skianyn Vannin (Manx airline) will take you there.
Tel: 08457 256256

761

X-RATING XXX

Cut up a scrapped car with an angle grinder.

As long as it is not your own car, have a go with a Bosch
GWS 20–230 9" 2,000-watt Angle Grinder.

762

X-RATING X

Do your food shopping over the Internet.

www.tesco.com will take your order and your payment on line, then
deliver your goods at your door in neat little Tesco plastic bags.

763

X-RATING X

Ride a bike from London to Brighton.

It's only 59.1 miles (94km).

764–773

Read ten classic fiction books –

764 *American Psycho* by Brett Easton Ellis — XXXXX

765 *The Wasp Factory* by Iain Banks — XXXXX

766 *Heart of Darkness* by Joseph Conrad — XXX

767 *The Diceman* by Luke Rhinehart — XXX

768 *On the Road* by Jack Kerouac — XXX

769 *The Black Dahlia* by James Ellroy — XXXXX

770 *Trainspotting* by Irving Welsh — XXXXX

771 *The Crab with the Golden Claws* by Hergé — X

772 *Will You Please Be Quiet, Please?* by Raymond Carver — X

773 *Lady Chatterley's Lover* by DH Lawrence — XXXX

774 X-RATING XX

Play Diplomacy.

That is, if you want to make life-long enemies of the other players and an instant split-up with your girlfriend. Could be just what you're looking for!

775 X-RATING X

Own a Nokia Communicator.

Full-colour screen with 4096 colors, mobile email, Word, spreadsheet, presentation viewer, high speed Internet access and WAP, mobile multimedia.
www.nokia.com.

776 X-RATING X

Ask your prospective in-laws what the details of the dowry are.

777

X-RATING XXXX

Have sex in the darkened room of a party with your girlfriend sitting on your knee.

778

X-RATING X

Own a lava lamp.

This quaint electrical appliance was invented by Mr Craven-Walker in 1963. Take the plunge and buy a 'Sputnik', a 'Jupiter 2' or a 'Fase 3' from www.mathmos.co.uk.

779

X-RATING X

Bowl a perfect game at a bowling alley.

A perfect game is 12 strikes and your score will be 300.

780

X-RATING XXX

Take off from a breezy beach with a stunt kite.

The Kite Shop Limited
PO Box 288
Southampton
Hampshire SO17 2XU.

781

X-RATING XXX

Have a go on a climbing wall.

Mile End Climbing Wall
Haverfield Road
Bow
London E3 5BE
or visit www.ep-uk.com to buy bolts you can screw on your dining room wall.

782

X-RATING XX

See Wagner's complete Ring cycle

The closest to sex you'll ever get while
fully clothed – the tango.

783 X-RATING XXX

Go skateboarding at the South Bank Centre.

Waterloo or Embankment Underground stations.

784 X-RATING XXX

Paddle a canoe up a river.

785 X-RATING XXX

Tango with a Latin beauty.

The Dance Holiday Company Ltd
12 Chapel Street North
Colchester
Essex C02 7AT
It doesn't promise the Latin beauty,
but you'll look less silly when you try to dance...

786–795

See the top ten war movies –

786 *The Longest Day* (1962) **XXX**

787 *The Great Escape* (1963) **XX**

788 *Bridge on the River Kwai* (1957) **XXX**

789 *Saving Private Ryan* (1998) **XXXXX**

790 *Cross of Iron* (1977) **XXXXX**

791 *Full Metal Jacket* (1987) **XXXXX**

792 *All Quiet on the Western Front* (1930) **XXXX**

793 *Apocalypse Now* (1979) **XXXXX**

'Saigon.
Shit.
I'm still only in Saigon.
Every time I think I'm gonna wake up back in the jungle.'

794 *A Bridge Too Far* (1977) **XXX**

795 *Zulu* (1964) **XXXX**

796

X-RATING XX

Attend the Pan-African Film Festival in
Ouagadougou, Burkina Faso.

The next FESPACO will be on February 22 to March 1, 2003. Information:
01 BP 2505
Ouagadoudou
01 Burkina Faso.

797

X-RATING X

Get your photograph in *Alaska Men* magazine.

798

X-RATING X

Visit Jim Morrison's grave in Paris.

Jim Morrison moved to Paris in March 1971 to devote himself to writing.
He was found dead in his bath on July 3, 1971. He is buried in the
'Quartier des Poètes' in the Cimetière du Père-Lachaise, 75019, Paris.

799

X-RATING XXX

Fire a .357 Magnum at a US gun club.

800   X-RATING **XXX**

Ride a Baja Bug in Baja California.

A Baja Bug is the cool-looking, fat-tyred Volkswagen Beetle with the boot sliced away, exposing a 'hot' engine.

801   X-RATING **XXX**

Check out the women-to-men ratio in Caracas (8-to-1).

802   X-RATING **X**

Sell your old crap at a car boot sale.

803   X-RATING **XXXXX**

Smoke a 10-skin reefer.

804

X-RATING **XXX**

Ask your least favourite TV presenter for a signed photograph.

805

X-RATING **X**

Own a Panasonic portable DVD player.

www.panasonic.com.

806

X-RATING **XXX**

Take a helicopter flight over the Grand Canyon.

Papillon Grand Canyon Helicopters will guide you on a 50-minute flight above this extraordinary geological site for $164 (£120) per person. www.papillon.com.

807

X-RATING **X**

Have a go on a drum kit.

808-817

Watch ten TV classics –

808	*League of Gentlemen*	XXXXX
809	*Fawlty Towers*	XX
810	*South Park*	XXXX
811	*Spaced*	XXX
812	*This Life*	XXXXX
813	*The Simpsons*	XXX
814	*Charlie's Angels*	X
815	*Monty Python's Flying Circus*	XXX
816	*Baywatch*	XXX
817	*Buffy the Vampire Slayer*	XXX

818

X-RATING X

Go jogging with a CD walkman.

819

X-RATING XXX

Drink a Bishop's Finger.

Produced by Shepherd Neame (www.shepherd-neame.co.uk),
the oldest brewery on the UK (founded in 1698),
it is available in casks (5.0%) or bottles (5.4%).

820

X-RATING XX

Have a fondue in Switzerland.

Easy to prepare: bung Gruyere cheese and white wine in a pan, put the pan
over a gas burner in the middle of a dining table, stick pieces of bread on
long forks and dip in. Pretty messy, but fun for forfeits when you
drop your cheese (so to speak).

821

X-RATING XXXXX

Remove a woman's underwear with your teeth.

822

X-RATING X

Own a pair of Carhartt jeans.

Shotgun Clothing
Sunset Walk
Milton Keynes Shopping Centre
Milton Keynes
Buckinghamshire
Tel: 01908 677746.

823

X-RATING X

Go to a Gaelic football match in Co. Kerry.

Stay in style while over there:
Glenduff House
Kielduff
Tralee
County Kerry
Republic of Ireland.

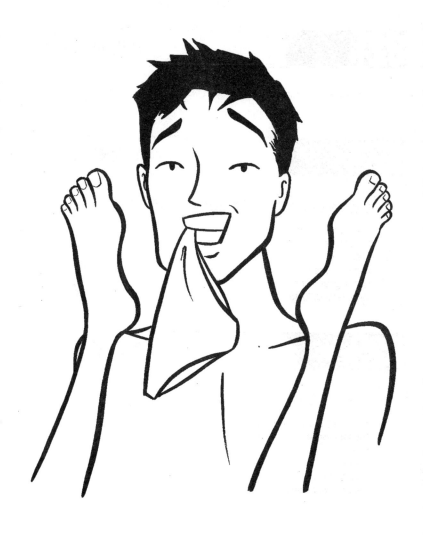

"Phew! Just don't ask me to put them back on!"

824 — X-RATING **XX**

Catch a fish and eat it by the sea (cook it first).

825 — X-RATING **XX**

Get your secretary to ask if she can use your Dictaphone.

826 — X-RATING **XXX**

Spend a night in a haunted house.

http://pages.zoom.co.uk/hauntedplaces lists haunted houses available for you to visit as well their history.

827

X-RATING XXXXX

See a Tasmanian Devil in the flesh.

These beasts have jaws of biting power as strong as a dog roughly 4 times their weight, so be careful. Popular viewing in Tasmania (funnily enough) Mt Williams National Park.

828

X-RATING XXXX

Pick up a hitchhiker.

829

X-RATING XXXX

Take a boat trip underneath Niagara Falls.

*Whirlpool Jet
PO Box 1215
Niagara On the Lake
Ontario L0S 1J0
Canada
www.whirlpooljet.com.*

830   X-RATING XXX

Get into the *Guinness Book of Records*.

831   X-RATING X

Take the EuroStar to Paris.

Three hours from London to Paris from Waterloo Station. Go to your local rail station or travel agent or telephone: 0870 160 6600.

832   X-RATING X

Own a pair of Adidas Predator football boots.

www.adidas.com.

833   X-RATING XXX

Spend an Evening in Hamburg.

A flight from London Stansted (STN) to Hamburg, Germany (HAM) will cost you around £100. Try:
www.buzzaway.com.

834

X-RATING XXXX

Climb a mountain in the Andes.

Sherpa Expeditions
Tel: 020 8577 7187.

835

X-RATING X

Convert your vinyl collection to CDs.

836

X-RATING X

Own a philosophy football t-shirt.

837

X-RATING X

Wear a Frankie Says… t-shirt.

838

X-RATING **X**

Own a DVD writer.

839

X-RATING **XX**

Visit Angkor Wat in Cambodia.

Angkor Wat is the largest religious monument in the world. This huge pyramid temple was built by Suryavarman II between 1113 and 1150. It is surrounded by a moat 570 feet wide and about four miles long.

840

X-RATING **XXXX**

Have sex with a follower of all the world's major religions.

841

X-RATING **XXX**

Go paint-balling with your work mates and shoot your boss.

Play Village Siege, Blisterball, Protect the President or Fort Invasion at:
Paint Zone
Salmons Lane
Whyteleafe
Surrey
Tel: 07899 831782.

842

X-RATING XX

Cuddle up by a fire in the Mull of Kintyre.

843

X-RATING XX

Get an audience with the Pope.

*This could prove to be difficult, but you can still
check out on the Pope by visiting www.vatican.va.*

844

X-RATING XXXXX

Go to an Istanbul derby match.

Galatasaray, Fenerbahce, Besiktas and Istanbulspor all play in Istanbul.

845

X-RATING XXXXX

Get close to ancient gods by climbing Mount Olympus.

*The highest peak in the Olympic Mountains, Mount Olympus rises
7,965 ft and was first sighted by the English explorer John Meares
in 1788. The mountain of the Gods is not that difficult to climb, but
beware of the unstable weather: Mt Olympus does claim lives every year.*

"I'd like a couple of those, please."

846 X-RATING **XX**

Eat sheep's eyeballs in a Yurt in Mongolia.

847 X-RATING **XX**

Go snorkelling on the Great Barrier Reef.

848 X-RATING **XX**

Be served by a buxom wench at a Tudor banquet.

849 X-RATING **X**

Drink Sapporo in Sapporo.

The best time to go would be during the Sapporo Snow Festival, when hundreds of ice sculptures are carved and displayed before melting away.

850–859

X-RATING

Read ten classic non-fiction books –

850   *The Joy of Sex* by Dr Alex Comfort   **XXXXX**

851   *The Consolations of Philosophy* by Louis de Botton   **XX**

852   *World War I* by John Keegan   **XX**

853   *World War II* by John Keegan   **XX**

854   *Flat Back Four* by Andy Gray   **X**

855   *The Art of War* by Sun Zhou   **XXXX**

856   *Addicted* by Tony Adams   **XXX**

857   *My Last Breath* by Luis Buñuel   **XXX**

858   *Essays and Aphorisms* by Schopenhauer   **XXX**

859   *Only a Game* by Eamon Dunphy   **X**

860

X-RATING XX

Go a whole day without talking (you may as well practice for wedded 'bliss').

861

X-RATING XXX

Go fly-posting.

'Bill Posters will be Prosecuted!'

862

X-RATING X

Own a satellite phone.

863

X-RATING XXXX

Offer to 'cure' a lesbian.

864   X-RATING **X**

Own a Sony AIBO robot dog.

The new second generation AIBO (ERS-210) has an integrated camera in its eyes and you can download the images on to your computer to watch them. It also recognises 50 English words, it can even dance and run.
www.us.aibo.com

865-874   X-RATING

Tell an Essex girl joke –

865   How does an Essex girl turn   **XXXX**
off the light after sex?
She shuts the car door.

866   What does an Essex girl   **XXXXX**
say after sex?
"Do you all play for the same team?"

867   Why do Essex girls   **XXXXX**
wear underwear?
To keep their ankles warm.

868   What's the difference between   **XXXXX**
an Essex girl and a toilet?
A toilet doesn't follow you around
when you've used it.

869 What do you call an Essex girl with half a brain?
Gifted.

XXX

870 What do a headlight and an Essex girl have in common?
They both get screwed on the front of Ford Escorts.

XXXX

871 What do an Essex girl and a moped have in common?
They're both fun to ride until your mates catch you.

XXXX

872 What is an Essex girl's definition of safe sex?
Locking the car door first.

XXX

873 How many Essex girls does it take to change a lightbulb?
What's a lightbulb?

XX

874 What does an Essex girl use to keep her ears warm?
Her ankles.

XXXX

875 X-RATING **XXX**

Go deer-hunting in the Rockies.

876 X-RATING **XXXX**

Have one off the wrist at work. During office hours.

877 X-RATING **XXX**

Go to Iceland for the pure-bred blondes.

The Embassy of Iceland in London
2a Hans Street
London SW1X 0JE.

878 X-RATING **XXX**

Use a pair of binoculars for some *Rear Window* activity.

879 X-RATING **XXXXX**

Hide in a cupboard when her husband/boyfriend comes home.

880

X-RATING XXXXX

Have a sex session with a woman in suspenders.

881

X-RATING XXXXX

Do a 'Marianne Faithful' – sponsored by Mars.

882

X-RATING XXXX

Make a 'donation to the National Trust'.
(Dump in the open air).

Or do it the right way and become a member:
NT Membership Department
P O Box 39
Bromley
Kent BR1 3XL
Tel: 020 8315 1111.

883

X-RATING XXX

Eat Bombay Duck.

884

X-RATING **XXX**

Go to a non-league football match.

885

X-RATING **XXX**

Fish with a spear.

886

X-RATING **XX**

Stick a prawn on a barbie in Perth.

That's Western Australia, not Scotland.

887

X-RATING **XXXX**

Photocopy your arse at the office party.

This is not a very arduous task... The hard bit is to prevent one of the 400 copies reaching your boss's desk before morning.

888

X-RATING **XXXXX**

Use a Polaroid for the obvious reasons.

Polaroid 600 Extreme plus 10-exposure film: £24.25.

"That's 400 copies, please, Miss Jones."

889
X-RATING XX

Smoke a Havana in Cuba.

890
X-RATING XXX

Parade in Red Square.

Bang in the middle of Moscow, next to the Kremlin, Red Square is much more open to the public than it used to be.

891
X-RATING XXX

Throw a water bomb out of an upstairs window.

892
X-RATING XXXXX

Wake up with no recollection of the previous 48 hours.

893
X-RATING XXX

Paddle down a river in a barrel.

894

X-RATING XXXXX

Surf the Internet 'left-handed'.

Visit www.yahoo.com and type 'sex'. You'll be busy for hours (in April 2001, there were 2,420,000 web page matches). A search of altavista.com for 'sex' realised 'about 18,493,994' web sites.

895

X-RATING XXXXX

Join in an orgy.

896

X-RATING XXXXX

Swim in a shark cage.

897

X-RATING XX

Drink a stubby in an outback boozer.

898

X-RATING XXXX

Take a dip in the Ganges.

899 X-RATING XXXXX

Get caught 'perusing' a jazz mag by your prospective mother-in-law (she should know what she's signing up for!).

900 X-RATING XXX

Urinate in a receptacle other than a toilet or urinal.

901 X-RATING XXXXX

Go sky diving.

www.dirtdive.co.uk is a site that will give you all the details of the registered parachuting and skydiving clubs in Great Britain.

902 X-RATING XXX

Go to a pub on the middle of the moors.

903 X-RATING XX

Do not see any sunlight for seven days.

904

X-RATING XXXXX

Eat a banana 'the Amsterdam way' in front of an audience.

905

X-RATING XX

Grow a lumberjack beard.

906

X-RATING XXXXX

Audition for *The Annabel Chong Story II*.

Annabel Chong (Grace Quek) was the woman who instigated the world's biggest gangbang when she had sex with 251 men.

907

X-RATING XXX

Give up cigarettes – and take up pipe-smoking.

908

X-RATING XXXX

Melt an ice maiden.

909 X-RATING XXX

Go deep-sea fishing off the Cornish coast.

910 X-RATING XXXX

Receive instruction from a lassie in a Vivienne Westwood tartan mini skirt.

Vivienne Westwood
44 Conduit Street
London WIR 9FB
Tel: 020 7287 3188.

911 X-RATING XXX

Walk the length of the Great Wall of China.

We are talking a long walk here. The surviving sections of the Great Wall of China would, if put end to end, cover the distance from New York to Los Angeles! It is the only man-made structure on Earth to be visible from the Moon.

912 X-RATING XX

Have all of your body hair shaved off.

913

X-RATING XXX

Dress as a sheikh and shop in Harrods.

Harrods Limited
Knightsbridge
London SW1X 7XL.

914

X-RATING X

Visit the tomb of the Unknown Soldier.

Find it in Paris, under the Arc de Triomphe, Place de l'Etoile.

915

X-RATING X

Own a remote-controlled dune buggy.

916

X-RATING XX

Go busking.

917

X-RATING XXX

Fluff up a bunny girl's tail.

Don't forget the 'Kiss me – I'm Irish' badge.

918

X-RATING XX

Sell a story to a tabloid.

Telephone The Sun *direct on 020 7782 4100.*

919

X-RATING XX

Throw a dart at a map of England and drive to where it lands.

920

X-RATING XXX

Celebrate St Patrick's Day in New York.

921

X-RATING X

Email the President of the United States of America.

president@whitehouse.gov.

922

X-RATING XXXXX

Compete in the Iditarod husky-sledge race in Alaska.

Prepare yourself for the possibility that you'll never come back.

923 X-RATING XX

Smoke on a bus on the Continent.

924 X-RATING XX

Sell copies of *The Big Issue* to society birds in Sloane Square.

925 X-RATING XXX

Go on a Monopoly pub crawl of London.

926 X-RATING X

Own a Drizabone waterproof knee-length coat.

www.drizabone.com.au

927 X-RATING X

Visit Hitler's secret bunker.

Under the garden of the Reichskanzlei, which was at 77 Wilhelmstraße, in Berlin.

928

X-RATING XX

Take your boss out for lunch – to a greasy spoon.

929

X-RATING XXX

Play a league season of park football.

930

X-RATING XXX

Visit an Indian reservation.

The Navajo Nation is situated in Arizona.
Get a booklet about their government from:
Office of Navajo Government Development
PO Box 220
Window Rock
Arizona 86515 USA.

931

X-RATING XXX

Drive a Model T Ford.

932

X-RATING X

Clean a Premier League footballer's boots.

933

X-RATING XX

Take your nephew and his mates to the zoo
(it'll put you off kids for life).

*London Zoo should take care of that... The main gate is
situated on the Outer Circle of Regent's Park.*

934

X-RATING XX

Study to be a private detective.

Academy of Professional Investigation.
*Telephone: 01444 441111 for further information regarding their Distance
Learning courses for the Beginner.*

935

X-RATING XXX

Spend a whole day talking like Jar Jar Binks.

936

X-RATING X

Bet your shirt on a horse in the Grand National.

937

X-RATING X

Get a personalized number plate.

*You can use any letter or number on a number plate except Q.
www.regtransfers.co.uk will tell you everything you need to know
and let you perform a very exhaustive search online.*

938

X-RATING X

Have Bombay potatoes in Bombay.

939

X-RATING XXX

Spend a beery weekend in Prague.

940

X-RATING X

Own some Calvin Klein briefs.

*These are probably available down your local street market, otherwise visit
www.ukdesignershop.com.*

941

X-RATING XXX

Keep a woman's underwear in your pocket for a day.

942
X-RATING **XXXX**

Photograph yourself having sex in a photo booth.

943
X-RATING **XXXX**

Buy a dodgy video from a late-night sex shop.

944
X-RATING **XX**

Get steamed up in Death Valley.

Death Valley in California is the hottest place on Earth, where the ground can reach boiling point in summer (average temperature: 39°C). With names like Furnace Creek, Stovepipe and Badwater (282 feet below sea level), you'll do well to stay in your air-conditioned car.

945
X-RATING **XXX**

Hitch-hike from Paris to Nice.

946
X-RATING **X**

Own a PDA.

In case you didn't know, it is a palm-top computer/organizer.

947

X-RATING XX

Buy a Trabant in Eastern Europe and drive it back home.

The Trabant was the most famous mode of transport in Eastern Europe in the 50s (slightly bigger than a Gogomobil T300) and can be bought from German and Czech clubs if you speak the language.

948

X-RATING XXXX

Take an illegal tour of the Paris catacombs.

It is possible to visit more than the well-trodden bits of the French catacombs, as there are more than 187 miles of underground tunnels underneath Paris and plenty of entrances. To find your way around, go online and connect to http://riffzone.phpwebhosting.com/papote.

949

X-RATING XX

Watch *Jaws* and take your girlfriend for a midnight skinny-dip.

950

X-RATING X

Enter a raft race.

951
X-RATING XX

Pull a bird in a supermarket.

As long as it is not a frozen chicken, you're OK.

952
X-RATING X

Attend a famous author's book signing.

Check out the Book section in The Guardian *on Saturday or* Time Out.

953
X-RATING XX

Gatecrash a wedding reception.

954
X-RATING XX

Drive a tank.

Bovingdon Tank Museum
Dorset
Tel: 01929 405096.

Finding a parking place could prove tricky.

955
X-RATING **XXX**

Stay in the bridal suite of the Hilton.

Hilton London Green Park
Half Moon Street
London W1Y 8PB
Tel: 020 7629 7522.

956
X-RATING **XX**

Attend a party at the Roof Gardens in Kensington.

957
X-RATING **XXX**

Take a tour of the Falkland Islands.

958
X-RATING **X**

Own a Panama hat.

Edward Bates Ltd
21a Jermyn Street
St. James's
London SW1Y 6HP.

959

X-RATING XX

Go mountain biking in Utah.

960

X-RATING XXX

Fire an HKMP5.

And fit it with a LAW-17, the original factory integrated mini-laser aimer.

961

X-RATING XXX

Travel on the St Lawrence Seaway.

Connecting the Atlantic Ocean with the Great Lakes through Canada, it provides in excess of 9,300 miles of navigable waterways.

962

X-RATING XXXX

Spend a night in your car in a snowstorm.

963

X-RATING XX

Audition for a bit-part in a movie.

964 X-RATING XXXXX

Be an extra on Coronation Street.

Granada Television
Quay Street
Manchester M60 9EA
Tel: 0161 832 7211.

965 X-RATING XXXXX

Join the Masons.

www.grand-lodge.org.

966 X-RATING XXX

Run around a park with a rucksack full of bricks.

967 X-RATING XX

Own a punch bag.

968 X-RATING XX

Make a list of your sexual conquests.

969   X-RATING **XXXXX**

Play 'soggy biscuit' with your mates.

970   X-RATING **XXX**

Piss in a bottle on a long car journey.

971   X-RATING **XX**

Ride in a propeller plane.

972   X-RATING **X**

Burn your entire CD collection onto MP3 CDs.

Here is a guide: a regular album, once converted to MP3 format, will use roughly 50 to 60mb. A regular CD can hold 650mb of data. You will fit around 11 to 12 albums on one CD.

973   X-RATING **XXX**

Visit Machu Picchu.

Machu Picchu, the Sacred Valley in Peru, is the most famous Latin American attraction. It is set in the valley of the Urabamba and was built by the Pachacuti Indians.

"Free love? Well, I'm not paying!"

974

X-RATING XX

Create a commune.

975

X-RATING X

Get a question right on *University Challenge*.

976

X-RATING XXXXX

Shake hands with H.M. The Queen.

977

X-RATING XX

Work on a market stall for a day.

*Try your hand at Walthamstow Market, High Street,
Walthamstow, the longest outdoor market in Europe.*

978

X-RATING XXXXX

Frolic with a hippy chick at the Reading Festival.

*National Express operates special buses to the site:
Call 08705 80 80 80 for more info.*

979

X-RATING **XXXX**

Find a girl with a deft touch to loosen your belt.

980

X-RATING **X**

Grow dreadlocks.

981

X-RATING **XX**

Own a digital video camera with computer editing facility.

982

X-RATING **XX**

Wear a t-shirt with 'Italians Do It Better' on it.

983

X-RATING **XXXXX**

Visit Karl Marx's grave at Highgate cemetery.

There are about 167,000 people buried in the Cemetery in 52,000 graves, so don't get lost.

984

X-RATING XX

Go to sleep in one of the display beds at Ikea.

985

X-RATING XXXXX

Get into the MI5 building pretending to be a spy.

986

X-RATING XXX

Visit the Oracle at Delphi.

987

X-RATING X

Wear a 'Ming the Merciless' moustache for a day.

You can also pinch your skin and glue the parts together to create realistic scars.

988

X-RATING XXXX

Spend a week of sea, sun and… whatever in Zanzibar.

989

X-RATING **XXX**

Hang around in Harlem.

990

X-RATING **XXX**

Visit the Kremlin.

991

X-RATING **XX**

Own a Paul Smith suit.

Paul Smith
40–44 Floral Street
London WC2E 9DG.
Tel: 020 7836 7828.

992

X-RATING **XXXXX**

Have sex with a (female) soldier.

993
X-RATING X

Visit the Normandy landing beaches: Gold, Sword, Juno, Omaha and Utah.

European Battlefield tours at:
Leger Holidays
Canklow Meadows
Rotherham
South Yorkshire S60 2XR.

994
X-RATING X

Visit Bethlehem at Christmas.

995
X-RATING XXXX

Eat black pudding.

996
X-RATING XXXX

Take part in a pagan ritual.

The Pagan Book of Days: *a guide to the festivals, traditions and sacred days of the year by Nigel Pennick. Paperback ISBN 0892813695.*

997

X-RATING XXXXX

Infiltrate an underground organization.

998

X-RATING XX

Stand to get elected in a general election.

999

X-RATING XX

Watch the All-Blacks play in New Zealand.

WestpacTrust Stadium
Wellington
New Zealand.

1000

X-RATING XXXX

Smoke it up on a Jamaican holiday.

1001

X-RATING XXXXX

Call off a wedding.